Southern Italy : An Archaeological Guide

Southern Italy:
An Archaeological Guide

the main prehistoric, Greek and Roman Sites

MARGARET GUIDO

NOYES PRESS
Noyes Building
Park Ridge, New Jersey 07656, USA

FOR JUDITH AND BILLY

'The dead were and are not. Their place knows them no more and is ours today. Yet they were once as real as we, and we shall tomorrow be shadows like them. In men's first astonishment over that unchanging mystery lay the origins of poetry, philosophy and religion.'

G. M. Trevelyan in *Clio, a muse & other essays.*

Contents

Illustrations

Acknowledgements

I am grateful to a number of colleagues for their help in providing me with illustrations for this book. They are acknowledged below and include particularly Prof. Giuseppe Foti, Soprintendente alle Antichità for Calabria, Prof. Lo Porto, Soprintendente for Apulia, Dr Geoffrey Woodhead and Messrs Thames and Hudson for kindly allowing me to reproduce a plan and photographs from *The Greeks in the West*, and Herr Thomas Günther.

Above all I particularly want to thank Professor Robert Cook of Cambridge University for patiently reading this book in typescript, and for correcting a number of errors: those that may remain are entirely my own.

For the illustrations I thank the following:
The Italian State Tourist Office (ENIT) for Plates 3, 5 and 10A. The Soprintendenza alle Antichità for Calabria for Plates 22, 23, 25 and 27. The Soprintendenza alle Antichità for Apulia for Plates 14 and 16. Messrs Alinari for Plates 4, 10B, 17, 24, 28 and 29. The Director of the Museum at Lecce for Plates 21A and 21B (the latter photograph by G. Guido). Dr Geoffrey Woodhead for the plan of Posidonia (Paestum) and Plates 15 and 31B. Fototeca Unione, Rome, for Plates 1, 2, 6, 7 and 12. Herr Thomas Günther (Hans Gunther Verlag, Stuttgart) for Plates 9, 26 and 31A.

I am also grateful to Commander Paget for having taken me to Cumae and Baia, in spite of ill-health, and for allowing me to profit from his stimulating ideas.

MARGARET GUIDO

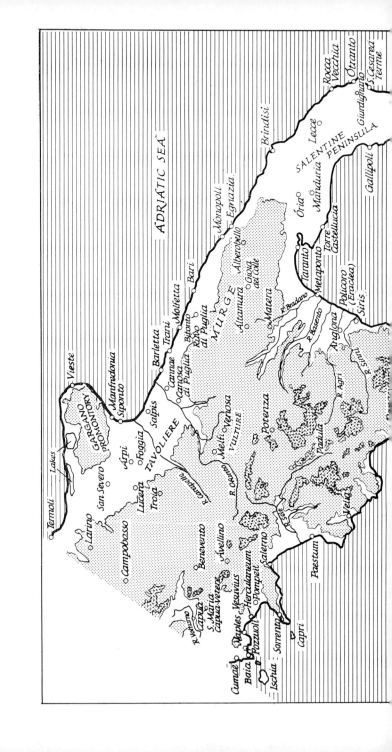

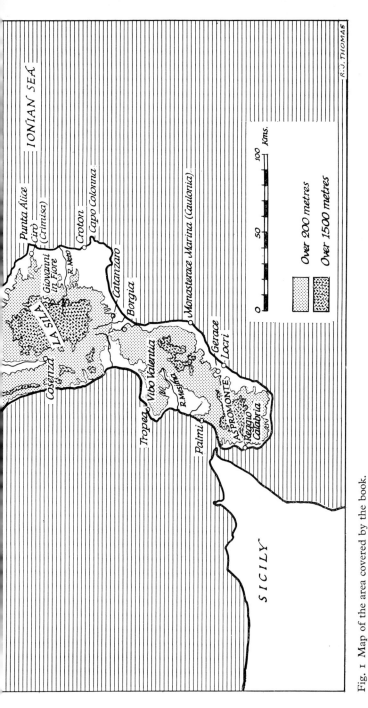

Fig. 1 Map of the area covered by the book.

INTRODUCTION

The area covered by this book is a very large and a very varied one, ranging from the islanded coast of Naples, the flat plain around Foggia, the gentle hilly country of central Apulia and the flatter land of the Salentine peninsula, the rugged and less accessible hills of Calabria and the Potenza area, and the narrow coastal strips of the Ionian and Tyrrhenian coasts where the first Greek settlements were established.

The book is arranged in six chapters, made up in such a way that each deals not with a geographical unit but with an area crossed by some major communication route: tourists therefore turn off to either side without the inconvenience of having to consult another map. Such a system has its disadvantages for it results in some very long and some short chapters. Another inequality in the book may be found in the number of monuments mentioned in the various chapters: in Calabria for instance—so often damaged by earthquakes, landslides and floods—the remaining early buildings of interest are relatively few and most have been mentioned if not described; in the Naples area on the other hand the patrimony of buildings of architectural merit is so vast that nothing outside the immediate period covered by this book, from prehistoric times to the end of the Roman period, has been mentioned. For every other aspect of human achievement, architecture, painting etc., another book or books should be used, and I should certainly recommend Peter Gunn's *Companion Guide to Southern Italy* (Collins) as the best.

Hotels. These are not mentioned at all in the guide-book. For there are so many in the Naples and coastal areas in the north of the territory that their listing would take up an unwarranted space. In the southern and less developed regions, hotels are springing up almost monthly to provide for the ever-increasing number of tourists. It has therefore been felt that the wisest course is to advise people to consult an up-to-date hotel guide, such as the Michelin guide or one provided by the *Touring Club Italiano.*

Museums. Many are in course of rearrangement and although the hours of opening are correct at the time of going to press it is never wise to place too much faith in these for they are often altered. Anyone particularly needing to visit a certain museum would be well advised to check with the local tourist office before going.

Chapters are arranged alphabetically and the sites described are underlined on the relative maps.

Maps. It is important that only the most recent road maps should be used, owing to the many newly constructed roads which are not included in the older ones. It is advisable to use contoured maps when possible.

Maps can generally be obtained from the *Touring Club Italiano* or at a C.I.T. or *Ente Provinciale per il Turismo* office in the bigger towns and principal bookshops. Some may also be obtained at garages. All the same to make sure of getting the best it is wiser to buy one before leaving the U.K. or U.S.A., either at the Map House in St. James's Street, London, S.W.1, or at the Rizzoli International Bookstore, 712 Fifth Avenue, New York City.

Two useful maps are the *B.21. Campeggi e Villaggi Turisti in Italia*, and *B.96. Italia Meridionale* 1/500,000. More detailed maps are naturally necessary for field work. Some of the Touring Club maps also mark the Camping sites. The German maps are generally excellent.

Students needing assistance from the Soprintendententi alle Antichità should refer to the following places: Salerno for Campania, Reggio di Calabria for Calabria, Potenza for Basilicata, Taranto for Apulia and Naples for the Naples area. In many of the museums under the auspices of the Soprintendenze you need to make written application for a permit some time before you need to see the reserve collections which are not normally available to the public. Tickets giving free access to museums can be obtained by joining either *Italia Nostra* or the Italian Institute of Culture, in Belgrave Square, London, or 686 Park Avenue, New York City.

Method of travel. By far the most convenient way is by car, but the towns and coast roads are congested in the high season. To see the beauty of Calabria in particular a visit in late October can be recommended, and in fact October and May–June are perhaps the best months. November and December are made dangerous by blocked roads, floods or landslides after the autumn rains.

In Plans and Figures in this book I have often retained the Italian terms for greater facility on the sites.

I have not attempted to write an introductory essay to the prehistory and early history of Southern Italy, for space would not allow it, nor would our present knowledge. Rather than this I have written short introductory notes to each chapter, and have provided a chronological framework into which it is hoped the various monuments described in the text can be set for their historical background.

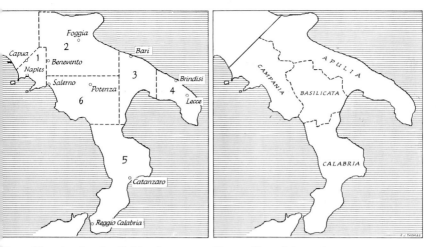

Fig. 2 Map showing the division into chapters.

Fig. 2A Map of the regions.

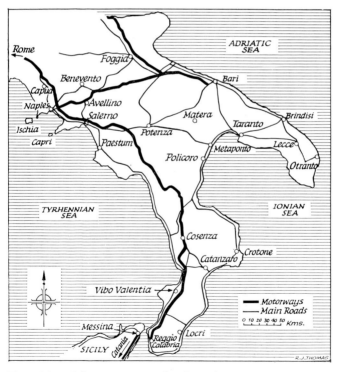

Fig. 3 Map of the motorways and main roads.

CHRONOLOGICAL NOTES

The earliest sites to be visited in the area covered by this book belong to the Upper Palaeolithic period of approximately 10,000 B.C. (there is a radio-carbon date of 9970 ± 580 B.C. for the Grotta Romanelli in the Salentine peninsula). For several thousand years after this our knowledge of South Italian prehistory is very vague, but by the VI millennium B.C. the earliest of the Neolithic cultures, apparently represented by pottery decorated with impressed designs, reached the area from the eastern Mediterranean, and we may reasonably expect that, though individual local groups of people were responsible for their own varieties of pottery decoration, the general sequence which followed is probably not very different, in the south and west at least, from that so clearly established for the Lipari Islands, and summarized in my *Sicily: an Archaeological Guide*. But the area is large, more cultural overlapping is to be expected, the proximity of Apulia to the other side of the Adriatic led to more frequent exchanges, and we need much more excavation before a clear picture can emerge. As a general guide the following dates can serve.

B.C.	
VI–III millennia	Neolithic cultures.
c. 2500	Copper Age begins and leads into
c. 2000–1450	Early Bronze Age.
c. 1450–1250	Middle Bronze Age.
c. 1250– 950	Late Bronze Age. During the whole of the Bronze Age, and perhaps particularly during its middle and later stages when the so-called Apennine and sub-Apennine cultures were developing greater homogeneity over most of the area, Southern Italy was open to a number of new contacts: from the Mycenaean world traders reached the Taranto district; Gaudo near Paestum was evidently culturally connected with Anatolia:

the Ótranto dolmens may have inspired or been inspired from the Maltese Tarxien Cemetery culture, and the Bari gallery graves reflect contact with the western megalithic culture which may have reached there via Sardinia. In addition the round cairns or 'specchie' of Apulia seem to share much with similar tombs in western Greece and the eastern Adriatic shores.

c. 950   Iron Age began.

At the end of the late Bronze Age and before the Greek colonization in the south, proto-Villanovan and then Villanovan commercial links were established sporadically, though the Villanovans (who possibly may have been proto-Etruscans) penetrated well down the western coast. To trade with their successors the Etruscans, the Greeks established their first colonies at Pithekoussai (Ischia) and Cumae in the Naples area. The next step was to guard the Messina Straits and then to colonize the coasts of the south and west of the mainland, and Sicily. The Euboeans and Corinthians went to Ischia, Cumae and Rhegion (Reggio Calabria); the Achaeans from the north-west Peloponnese, to Sybaris, Croton, Caulonia, Metapontum and Poseidonia (Paestum); and Spartans and others to Taras (Taranto) Siris, Locri, Velia etc. At the time when the Greeks founded their colonies, Southern Italy was inhabited by peoples collectively known as Bruttians (in Calabria), Lucanians (in the country centred on Potenza and roughly corresponding with modern Basilicata), Samnites (in the upland country around Benevento and further north) and three groups of Iapygians in Apulia: the Daunians in the north, the Peucetians in the centre, and the Messapians in the Salentine peninsula (the 'heel').

B.C.	
VIII or early VIIc	Pithekoussai, Rhegion, Cumae, Sybaris, Taras, Croton and Metapontum founded.
early VII c.	Locri founded.
VI c.	Hipponium and other colonies founded.
550–530	The 'Basilica' at Paestum built.
c. 540	Velia (*Elea*) founded.
late VI c.	Pythagorean school at Croton and Eleatic school at Velia.
510	Sybaris destroyed by Croton.
	At about this time the Etruscans were venturing further south into the Naples area and their trade began to threaten that of the Greek coastal towns which had so far enjoyed the monopoly. The Etruscans were finally defeated off Cumae in 474 B.C. by Hieron I of Syracuse. After the battle their influence in the area faded away.
473	The Messapians from the 'heel' inflicted a severe defeat on the Greeks—according to Herodotus this was the greatest massacre of Greeks that he could remember.
450	Temple of Neptune at Paestum built.
	About this time the local imitation of imported Attic pottery began in various centres and became dominant after the defeat of Athens in the Peloponnesian War in 404.
444	Thurii founded. Herodotus was one of the colonists.
420	The Samnites succeeded in taking Cumae.
	By now all the Italic peoples were causing trouble to the Greeks.

B.C.

c. 380	Dionysius I of Syracuse took much of the toe of Italy as well as towns here and there up the east coast.
early IV c.	Thurii fell, and the Lucanians pushed south and westwards into Calabria. By now Roman power was increasing, and when the people of Capua needed help against the Samnites, they pleaded to Rome.
343–341	*First Samnite War.*
327	*Second Samnite War* (Rome allied with the Apulian peoples).
321	Rome defeated by the Samnites at the battle of the Caudine Forks.
304	Roman-Samnite peace. Campania under Roman hegemony. Samnites relinquished claims to territorial expansion.
298–290	*Third Samnite War.* Final submission of the Samnites who were obliged to supply troops to the Romans.
(312)	(First stretches of the Via Appia built as a military road.)
281–280	The threat to the Greeks was now coming from the Romans, and Taras (Taranto) begged for military assistance from Pyrrhus, King of Epirus. Pyrrhus formed an alliance with the Messapians, Lucanians and Bruttians against Rome, but in 278 a new treaty was made between Rome and Carthage.
275	Pyrrhus, defeated by the Romans at Benevento, retired from Italy.

B.C.	
272	By now almost the whole of South Italy was in Roman hands and Taras also surrendered.
270	Rhegion (Reggio Calabria) taken by Rome.
268	The Via Appia was extended southwards, and continued by stages to link Capua with Brundisium (Brindisi).
264–241	*First Punic War*. Rome and Carthage fought to possess Sicily and its rich Greek colonial towns.
218–202	Hannibal crossed the Alps and the *Second Punic War* was fought.
216	Battle of Cannae. Great Roman defeat by Hannibal. The Samnites, Lucanians and Bruttians defected from Rome, but Carthage failed to send support to Hannibal.
212	Hannibal took Tarentum. (Greek Taras).
207	Hannibal defeated at Grumentum and shortly afterwards left Italy, and was finally defeated in Spain by Scipio Africanus.
132	The Via Popilia built to join Capua with Rhegion via Salerno, Cosenza and Hipponium.
103	Slaves Revolt in Campania. Growing unrest of the Italic peoples under Roman rule.
90–88	*Social (or Italic) wars*. Italic peoples finally granted Roman citizenship.
83	Sulla masters Southern Italy.
80–31	Intermittent civil disorders.

B.C.	
73–71	The Slaves' rebellion led by Spartacus. Defeated by Pompey.
70–8 B.C.	Three of the great writers living at this period in this area: Virgil (70–19 B.C.); Horace, born at Venusia (65–8 B.C.); Livy (59 B.C.–A.D. 17).
27	Augustus Caesar founded the Roman Empire.
A.D.	
54–68	Nero. (Seneca satirized the corrupt life of the period.)
61	St. Paul landed at Pozzuoli.
75	Vespasian built amphitheatre at Pozzuoli.
79	Destruction of Pompeii and Herculaneum by eruption of Vesuvius. The elder Pliny died.
95	The Via Domitiana restored and its course altered to link Cumae with Baia and Pozzuoli, and later continued down the west coast to south of Velia where it joined the Via Popilia.
114–117	Trajan's Arch at Benevento marked the start of the Via Traiana to Brindisi—a road designed to carry men and commercial goods to and from the eastern Mediterranean. Under Trajan the Roman Empire reached its greatest territorial expansion.
? 55–117	Life of the historian Tacitus.
117–138	Hadrian. The dates of later Roman emperors are given in the text.
476	Fall of the Western Roman Empire.

Greek Pottery Styles

c. 1050 B.C.	Proto-Geometric period begins.
c. 900 B.C.	Geometric period.
c. 720 B.C.	Archaic period.
c. 480 B.C.	Classical period.

ATTIC		CORINTHIAN	
c. 700 B.C.	Proto-Attic.	*c.* 720 B.C.	Protocorinthian.
c. 600 B.C.	Attic Black-figure.	*c.* 625 B.C.	Early Corinthian.
		600 B.C.	Middle Corinthian.
c. 530–425 B.C.	Attic Red-figure.	575 B.C.	Late Corinthian.

MUSEUMS

The big national collections are at Naples, Taranto and Reggio Calabria. The many other museums, including new ones at Paestum, Crotone, Policoro (Eraclea) etc., and innumerable other collections, are separately mentioned in the index.

1 · NAPLES AND ITS SURROUNDINGS

Agnano Terme, Bacoli, Baia, Capri, Capua, Castellamare di
Stabia, Cumae, Herculaneum, Ischia, Lake Avernus, Literno,
Naples (*Museo Archeologico Nazionale*), Nocera, Nola, Pompeii,
Pozzuoli, Santa Maria Capua Vetere, Sorrento, Vesuvius.

The description of Naples, an important Greek town, first founded
as *Neapolis*, in about the VII century B.C., is here limited to a description
of the *Museo Archeologico Nazionale*, perhaps the richest collection of
Greek and Roman antiquities in Europe.

The chapter also includes the various sites (Agnano Terme, Bacoli,
Baiae, Cumae, Lake Avernus and Pozzuoli) in the area to the north-west
of Naples, known as the Phlegraean Fields, as well as those on the slopes
of Vesuvius (Herculaneum, Pompeii, Castellamare di Stabia, etc.) and
in the Sorrento peninsula. A little further inland there are a few other
towns of archaeological interest, notably Santa Maria Capua Vetere,
while behind lies Benevento, the heart of the upland country inhabited
at the time of the earliest Greek colonies at Ischia and Cumae by
Samnites, against whom the Romans had to wage several wars before
they could establish themselves once and for all in the Naples area.

The natural harbours in the coastline falling within this chapter have
led to occupation from very early times. Capri is well known for its
particular variety of painted Neolithic pottery; Ischia was perhaps the
earliest of the Greek colonies in Italy; the commercial activities of the
Etruscans and their predecessors and perhaps ancestors, the Villanovans, reached down at least to the Sorrentine peninsula. Yet in spite of
intense maritime activity from early times, the remains described in this
chapter belong to the Greeks and Romans and reflect an artistic and
cultural level unsurpassed in early Europe.

After a short introduction to the various regions, the sites described
in this chapter are arranged, as in the following chapters, in alphabetical
order.

The Phlegraean (or 'flaming') *Fields* (Campi Flegrei) are so called
because of the burning lava which has periodically erupted from the
now apparently extinct volcanoes in the area. The district is formed of
gently undulating and luxuriant hills studded with trees, and lakes
which have formed in the water-filled craters: one of these is the

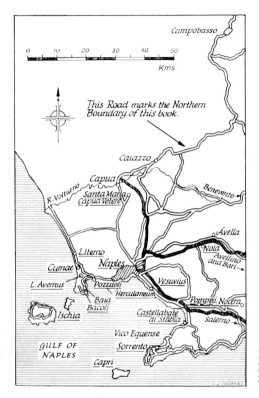

Fig. 4 Map of the Naples area and the Sorrento peninsula.

renowned Lake Avernus. The coast is beautiful with its transparent blue sea, its headlands, bays and off-shore islands—one of the loveliest coasts in Europe and one which through the course of history has been constantly altering owing to the effects of bradyseism—volcanic action which brings about a change in the relative height of land and sea. In Roman times, for instance, the land once sank sixteen feet in a few days and no Latin author bothered to mention it, and recently, in Bacoli, a rise of a centimetre a day has been recorded: it stands to reason, therefore, that the shore line in Greek and Roman times was very different from that of today; nor in such a strange land is it surprising to find that it has given rise to numerous legends going back to the time of the first Greek settlers at Cumae and Ischia, and handed down to us by Virgil and others. Here was the deep and mysterious Lake Avernus, in ancient times thought to be the entrance to the Infernal Regions visited by Hercules, Aeneas and Ulysses, and more revered still was the Cave of the Sibyl at Cumae whose oracular sayings were respected throughout the Greek world.

The volcanic disturbances also gave rise to various springs of medicinal waters whose properties were increasingly exploited by the Romans, so that in late republican and in imperial times the whole area was keenly sought after by rich Romans in retirement, in spite of frequent earthquakes which, the younger Pliny wrote to his friend Tacitus the historian, 'are so common in the Campania that we take no notice of them'. Baia particularly became a highly popular residential centre with numerous bath establishments frequented by people from all parts of the Empire. It must be remembered that in Roman times the Greek past of the Naples and Cumae district was very far from forgotten and many of the people were bilingual. So it was fashionable for writers and poets to turn from the Roman ideal of order, method and duty to the Greek love of beauty and contemplation for their inspiration. Virgil, 'poet of herdsmen, farms and heroes', was perhaps the greatest of these. Though born in Mantua he chose to live in Naples and near here he wrote the *Georgics* and part of the *Aeneid* at the very end of the I century B.C., and because he loved this land so much he chose a place for his tomb, now unfortunately lost, 'outside Naples on the road to Puteoli (Pozzuoli) between the first and second milestones'.

The whole area was the scene of intense building activity for hundreds of years under the Romans, and emperors and distinguished men in all fields of life frequented it.

Agnano Terme (Roman bath buildings)

A short distance to the north of the main Naples–Pozzuoli road, these buildings (*Terme Romane*) are laid out on six terraces one above the other. They have been so re-handled at various subsequent dates that they hardly merit a special visit by people who intend to see the much more spectacular bath-buildings at Baia.

Bacoli

There are several interesting remains here of the Roman town of *Bauli*. The Cento Camerelle, on two stories, are the huge reservoirs of one of the earliest and most well-known villas. The upper level, built in the 1st century A.D., consists of four parallel and intercommunicating cisterns, while the lower level belongs to the republican period. (Very near here was once Quintus Hortensius's villa which later belonged to Nero and then to the Flavians.)

The Piscina Mirabile is the largest known Roman water tank and is of spectacular proportions. To see it you should apply to Via A.Greco 16. It was made at the beginning of the Augustan period to ensure an adequate water supply for the fleet at Cape Misenum. Fed from a large aqueduct, it was provided with a system for purifying the water.

Baiae (Italian *Baia*)

Like all the surrounding neighbourhood, Baiae has been subjected to violent volcanic action, and as a result of the accompanying changes in the water level many important buildings may now lie under the sea. The town was famous in antiquity for the variety of its medicinal waters which Pliny extolled as 'the richest on earth'. Towards the later part of the republican period it began to become increasingly popular as a residential spa, and it has been said that 'men who possessed half a province elsewhere, contended here for a single acre.' In fact all around this bay which Horace claimed to be 'the most delightful in the world' emperors and other rich Romans (Caesar, Pompey, Varro, Cicero and many others) built themselves sumptuous villas and palaces. Strabo wrote 'palace after palace has been built at Baiae . . . a new city has grown up, in no way inferior to Puteoli (Pozzuoli).' It was here, too, that Caligula built one of his more extravagant follies—a road on a sort of pontoon bridge, designed to shorten the distance between Baiae and Pozzuoli.

The town is well known today for its very imposing and grandiose complex of Roman bath buildings—three separate but co-ordinated units built at different dates in the imperial period, and providing not only bathing facilities, but also sun-rooms, recreation rooms and even residential quarters. *The Terme Baiane*, as these buildings are called, have an entrance reached either from the Cumae road or from a stairway leading from the left of the station (*Stazione della Ferrovia Cumana*). Just behind this station is another bath building known as the *Temple of Diana*, of octagonal plan with a conical roof.

Those of the main complex, on the higher part of the hillside, called after Sosandra, Mercury and Venus, are open from 9 until dusk. These bath buildings have been made on the site of much earlier buildings on

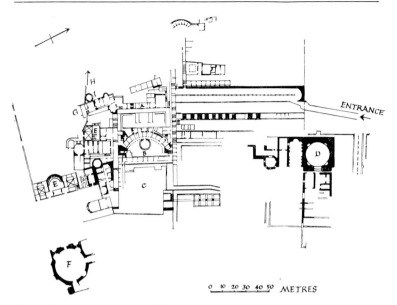

Fig. 5 Plan of Roman Bath buildings at Baia.

the upper level, destroyed by earthquakes. Three extremely interesting
but as yet little-understood structures remain in the north-west corner
of the complex. These are in Fig. 5 (G) an early temple, (I) a tholos once
perhaps free standing, and beside it—running for 120 metres into the
hillside and now only followed with difficulty—a long narrow corridor
cut into the rock (H) which some scholars think may in fact be the
renowned entrance to the Underworld (see Lake Avernus). The temple
foundations are very early, perhaps VI century; the passage is provided
with over 500 lamp niches and has an inner sanctuary reached by a
stair. When one realizes that the bath buildings are made in the side
of a volcanic crater, whose floor was where the lower thermal establishments can be seen, one cannot lightly dismiss the possibility that this
may have been Strabo's ancient oracle of the dead.

Terme di Sosandra, named after a fine marble copy of a V century
Greek bronze statue of Sosandra, contained on its upper level (A)
rooms dedicated to recreation and living apartments. The middle
part (B) was again designed for enjoyment, and specially adapted for

theatrical performances and music, while on the lower terrace (C) was the great bath itself with various rooms beneath it.

Terme di Mercurio (D). This was a large circular hall covered with a cupola inset with windows and open to the sky. It has been claimed that this building dates from early in the reign of Augustus: such an early date would give it an outstanding architectural importance, since it would antedate the Pantheon in Rome, which, though originally built by Agrippa, in its existing form mainly belongs to the time of Hadrian. However, on various grounds, the Terme di Mercurio is more likely to have been built around the mid or late 2nd century A.D.

Terme di Venere (E and E).
This is arranged on several levels and among its many rooms contains a nymphaeum with a fountain. Although entered separately, the so-called *Tempio di Venere* (F) really belongs to this group. It is octagonal outside and circular inside, with a vaulted roof and round-headed windows—a form of architecture characteristic of Hadrian's reign.

Capri

This island, world famous for its natural beauty, is chiefly of interest to archaeologists for its very early cave, known as the Grotta dei Felci, and for the once magnificent villa built for his own use by Tiberius, the *Villa Iovis*.

Geologically Capri is a continuation of the Sorrentine peninsula. Though first occupied in Palaeolithic times, its main contribution of significance to South Italian prehistory is provided by the late Neolithic painted wares, in the so-called 'Capri style', which were first recognized in the Grotta dei Felci on the slope of Monte Solaro. This pottery is decorated with bands and flame-like designs outlined in black, and is quite different from the spiral and meander decoration of the succeeding Neolithic period called Serra d'Alto after a site not far from Matera. The cave was also occupied during the Bronze Age.

Although Capri is thought to have been settled by Greeks, the earliest evidence does not go back before the V or IV century B.C. It was really the Romans who exploited the possibilities offered by this lovely island. Augustus visited it in 29 B.C. and lived there on several occasions until shortly before he died. His successor Tiberius, however, lived there much more continuously, and apparently built about twelve villas, of which the most famous, on the slopes of a precipitous rock

300 metres high, at Santa Maria del Soccorso, is the *Villa Iovis* whose name is recorded by Suetonius and also mentioned by Pliny. This, like the other remaining villas, has been sadly looted by unscientific diggers, and all the statuary and beautiful objects dispersed. The site is still worth visiting for its dramatic position and for the possibility it offers one to imagine the Emperor's lonely life there, for it was written, 'Even when Tiberius had quite defeated Sejanus's conspiracy, he felt so little reassured that for the next nine months he never left the villa.'

There is another much-damaged villa, the *Villa Imperiale Romana*, in Anacapri.

Capua

Capua falls within the area covered by the Archaeological Guide to *Central Italy*, but being so close to Santa Maria Capua Vetere, a few words must be said about it here. The town was built at a point where the Via Appia crossed a bend in the Volturno river, and this gave it a strategic military importance. There is a very important museum, the *Museo Campano*, and the Duomo contains Roman sarcophagi. Some Corinthian columns and bas-reliefs from the Amphitheatre at Santa Maria Capua Vetere (see p. 80) are incorporated in the Campanile.

Castellamare di Stabia (ancient *Stabiae*)

Two Roman villas can be visited here (though facilities are not always available), and it is best to ask first at the *Antiquarium Stabiano*, where there is an interesting collection.

The origins of the site go back to proto-historic times, and in fact the earliest finds from the necropolis date from the VIII century B.C. Its plural name suggests that it was once a number of small settlements rather than only one.

The necropolis is interesting for two reasons, first because it contains pottery of Villanovan influence, and secondly because, unlike most burial places around this coast, it contains remarkably little Greek ware.

After the Samnites invaded the area, Stabiae became the harbour for *Nuceria* (Nocera), and at the time of the Samnite wars with the Romans it was made into a military port, and an *oppidum* whose exact position is still not known. After various vicissitudes in these wars it was eventually destroyed in 89 B.C. by the Romans who were quick to grasp the possibilities offered by such a site, and during late republican and early

3

imperial times they developed it as a climatic resort. By a strange piece of good fortune it was not, according to Seneca, much damaged by the earthquake of A.D. 62 which caused so much havoc at Pompeii and elsewhere, but it suffered heavily in the eruption of Vesuvius a few years later.

Most of the excavations of the last century were totally unscientific, and their scope was limited to robbing the villas of their more precious contents; but subsequent work has enabled much to be saved. Two villas may be visited, and many others were scattered here and there on the slopes overlooking the sea; in fact the land here was almost as much sought after by Romans in retirement as was the area to the north of Naples around Pozzuoli and the Phlegraean Fields.

Of the two villas, one, the *Villa di Arianna* (Ariadne), has 13 rooms and stands on a ridge overlooking the Grotta di San Biagio. It contains various mosaics and paintings of some importance. It is not very easy to find the way to this villa, so it is advisable to ask at the Antiquarium.

The other, *Villa Romana*, is reached by taking Via Nocera till after crossing the railway at the level crossing you reach Ponte di San Marco where you should ask for the Fattoria dello Ioio.

Both villas are worth visiting, but most people will be content to concentrate on the more accessible Pompeii and Herculaneum.

The Antiquarium Stabiano. Most of the material comes from the old excavations of the villas, and some of the paintings are of particular interest. There are also important finds from the early necropolis, mentioned above, ranging in date from about the VIII to the II century B.C.

Cuma (Latin *Cumae*, Greek *Kyme*) (see Fig. 6)

Before reaching Cumae you pass through the arch called the *Arco Felice* which spans a deep cutting made through the hill at the time of Domitian to allow his new road to link Naples, Pozzuoli and Cumae. A stretch of this road surface can be seen here. The brick-built, barrel-vaulted arch supports three small arches for a viaduct above it. Looking down from here over the sea and the acropolis of Cumae is a moving sight for students of the classics.

At the western end of the Phlegraean Fields and overlooking the sea, Cumae was until recent years regarded as the earliest of all the western Greek colonies, as indeed Strabo had claimed. Now, however, we think

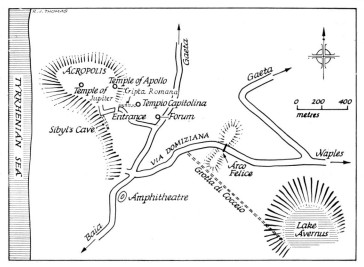

Fig. 6 Plan of Cumae and surroundings.

that as Livy stated *Pithekoussai* (Ischia) and possibly Syracuse and
Rhegion etc. slightly preceded it, though it was from Cumae that the
main flood of Greek influence reached the Etruscans and native peoples
to the north and east. Probably Greek traders, attracted by the metals
which were available further north, had already been prospecting along
the coast before they actually founded the colony. Then, in about the
mid VIII century B.C. the site of Cumae with its strong acropolis,
naturally defended by the sea, by woods, mountains and lakes, attracted
settlers from various parts of the Greek world, though mainly from
Pithekoussai and Euboea. As trade increased and the population multi-
plied, the Cumaeans founded *Neapolis* (Naples), a site which offered
the one thing so many of the earliest Greek colonies lacked, a good
harbour. The growing power of Cumae was watched with alarm by the
non-Greek peoples of the surrounding territory and they formed themselves into an alliance under the Etruscans who at that time had a
stronghold in Capua. To meet this threat, the Cumaeans in 474 B.C.,
begged assistance from Hieron I of Syracuse whose fleet engaged the
Etruscans off the coast and won so resounding a victory that it was
remembered for centuries and celebrated by Pindar. The famous helmet
in the British Museum, dedicated by Hieron at Olympia, recalls in its
inscription 'the Etruscan spoils won at Cumae'.

In spite of this success, it was only about fifty years later that Cumae fell into the hands of the Samnites, and it never achieved any great prosperity again until the Roman period when the whole area around the Phlegraean fields was much favoured for residential purposes and for the spa facilities which rich Romans developed around the mineral water springs.

The pottery from the tombs (now mostly in Room XXI of the *Museo Nazionale* in Naples) ranges over a long period beginning in at least the VII century B.C., and includes Protocorinthian and local Geometric wares as well as vases imported from Crete and the Cyclades. One mid-VII century lekythos bears the inscription 'I am Tataie's lekythos. May anyone who steals me be struck blind.' The first Attic wares reached Cumae in about 580, but once the town had passed into Samnite dominion the pottery was mostly Campanian, until the III century B.C. when this grew rare.

For the tourist the main attraction of the site is undoubtedly the Sibyl's Cave; for the historian, however, Cumae represents the point from which Greek culture was diffused into the relatively backward areas of the west. As Geoffrey Woodhead has put it, 'The tourist who visits the cave of the Virgilian Sibyl stands on ground more important for the development of the western world than he may perhaps realize.'

The main sites to visit are: the Amphitheatre, the so-called Sibyl's Cave, the *Cripta Romana*, the so-called *Tempio della Triade Capitolina*, the Acropolis with the Temple of Apollo, and the Temple of Jupiter, here described in that order.

The road leads to the foot of the acropolis which can be visited from 9 to 4, or 9 to 5 in summer. Note that most of the walls visible around the acropolis are of Roman date, but a few stretches of the V century B.C. (Samnite period) still exist. The only gateway was on the south near the Temple of Apollo.

The Amphitheatre, built outside the main precincts, is an early one, probably of the I century B.C.

The Sibyl's Cave. This was a sanctuary, greatly venerated throughout the Greek world from the VI or V century B.C. onwards. (See Plate 1.) Most of what you now see belongs to a slightly later date. It is generally said that the rectangular vaulted room at the end of the rock-cut gallery was where the prophetess or Sibyl sat on a high throne and made her

Plate 1 Cumae.
So-called Sibyl's
Cave.

oracular pronouncements. According to legend she was consulted by
Aeneas before he went down to the lower world to speak with the spirit
of his father Anchises. Her oracular sayings were written down, and the
last records of them to survive were destroyed when the Temple of
Jupiter on the Capitoline in Rome, where they were kept, was burnt.
Certainly this long corridor was regarded in Virgil's time, many centuries
after its construction, as the home of the Sibyl—'a vast cavern, a hundred
entrances and a hundred tunnels lead into it through which the Sibyl's
oracle emerges in a hundred streams of sound.' It seems more probable
that the real cave of the Sibyl has not yet been found and that this long
underground passage, modified at various times, was originally a
military work whose real date and significance we do not yet understand.

The Cripta Romana is the last stretch of the corridor cut by Cocceius for Agrippa, mentioned on p. 48.

Before going up to the acropolis you can see some 1st and 2nd century A.D. bath buildings (*Terme*) and the *Tempio della Triade Capitolina* (temple dedicated to Jupiter, Juno and Minerva); this is a building of imperial Roman date overlying an earlier one of the IV century B.C.

The Acropolis (Plate 2). Here are two temples, the lower of which is thought (from a dedicatory inscription in the Oscan language) to have been in honour of Apollo. But the building is not yet fully understood, and it is a palimpsest of different periods. The squared foundation blocks are of Greek or Samnite origin and they rest on foundations of a still earlier temple. The remains of columns etc. are of Augustan date or later, and the building was re-designed as a church in the early Christian period.

Plate 2 Cumae. General view of the Acropolis.

The Temple of Jupiter is an original Greek building of the V century B.C. and stands on the highest point. It was reconstructed under Augustus and then transformed into a 5-aisled Christian church in about the 6th century.

A great deal of research and new thinking needs to be done at Cumae. We are very far from understanding much about it at present.

Herculaneum (Plate 3) (Greek *Herakleion*) (Italian *Ercolano*)

To reach this site from Naples take either the Autostrada or the State road number 18 as far as Resina, and from there follow Corso Ercolano which leads to the excavated area. (Buses leave about every quarter of an hour from Naples; numbers 153 and 155 from Parco del Castello passing Piazza del Municipio, Corso Umberto and Corso Garibaldi.

Visiting hours are from 9 a.m. until an hour before dusk. The places of particular interest to those who cannot spend long are marked below with an asterisk. Some of the houses, almost all of which are named and numbered, are kept locked, but will be opened on request by one of the custodians. (The bold numbers refer to the numbers on the plan. Fig. 7. The others refer to the street numbers.)

Unlike Pompeii, Herculaneum was a relatively small town of only about 5,000 inhabitants, and it is in many ways easier to visualize in its Roman form than the larger and more commercial town not many kilometres away. If time allows you to visit only one of the two towns you would be well advised to go to Herculaneum which is quieter, less exhausting and equally, if not in some ways better, preserved. In a visit of two hours you can see all its main features.

It stood on a narrow promontory between two streams, and the grid layout of its streets suggests that it was originally a Greek town of the VI century B.C. probably under the hegemony of Naples and Cumae. But it then fell into the hands of the Samnites, and there are a few Oscan inscriptions belonging to this phase. In the I century B.C. it joined an alliance with other Italic towns against the Romans, but its stand was short-lived and it was taken in 89 B.C. and before long made a *municipium*. Its position below the slopes of Vesuvius, where the inhabitants cultivated their vineyards overlooking the sea, made the town particularly favoured for retirement in late republican and early imperial times, and many patrician men, distinguished for their services in various parts of the Empire, chose to live there, building themselves

Plate 3 View of Herculaneum.

Plate 4 Detail of mosaics in a house at Herculaneum.

substantial and elegant houses on two floors, often with internal court-yards and terraced gardens. One of the best-known citizens was Marcus Nonius Balbus, the proconsul whose equestrian statue is in the *Museo Nazionale* in Naples.

But their happiness did not endure. First came a serious earthquake in A.D. 62, necessitating widespread reconstruction (an inscription refers to a Temple of Mater Deum having been restored by Vespasian), and no sooner had this work been carried out than the disastrous eruption of A.D. 79 completely wiped out the town. As Tacitus wrote, 'the burning mountain of Vesuvius changed the face of the land and said to the sea "Be thou removed." '

Unlike Pompeii which was buried in hot cinders, Herculaneum was swallowed up in a mass of volcanic mud which solidified as it filled the streets and houses, and consequently many timber features such as tables and screens, as well as household objects (which were burnt at Pompeii), still remain to be seen today. The remains of the houses are striking for their luxury. They were mostly built and inhabited just at the most opulent moment in Roman times, a period whose material refinement has been described by Seneca in his 86th letter. He wrote, 'A man feels that he is a pauper and slovenly if his walls are not resplen-dent with huge expensive mirrors, if his marbles from Alexandria are not inlaid with slabs from Numidia, and if there is no border artistically worked around the entire circuit with a mosaic design . . . if the taps are not of silver . . .' etc. Surely these sumptuous houses were never again equalled until the Renaissance.

Excavations are still continuing, and much of the remaining part of the town, now under vineyards or condemned houses, will gradually be uncovered. Nearly all the finds are in the *Museo Nazionale* in Naples.

After the ticket office a long wide slope leads down to the excavated area. Since few people will want to follow a specific itinerary, the plan and short descriptions of the various buildings will enable them to select what they want to see. As is clear from the plan, in which the most important buildings are marked with a number, the sites flank the *Decumanus maximus* and the *Decumanus inferiore* and the three so-far excavated *Cardines* III, IV and V. You can enter from *Cardo* III. On the left at No. 2 is the *Casa d'Ago* (Argus's house) (**1**), so-called from a fresco no longer remaining, as it was badly excavated in the past. It was a large house with a peristyle and garden. On the opposite side of the narrow street at No. 3 is the *Casa del Scheletro* (House of the skeleton) (**2**) with a covered hall and two nymphaeums. Crossing the *Decumanus inferiore*

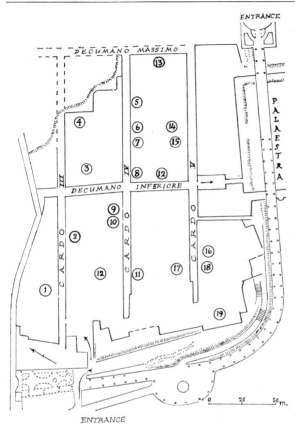

Fig. 7 Plan of Herculaneum showing most important buildings.

you next come to the *Terme*★ (bath buildings) (**3**) which occupy the whole space between *Cardo* III and IV. These were built in about 10 B.C. and were decorated rather later. Like the larger ones at Pompeii they were divided into separate quarters for men and women. Coming in from *Cardo* III you reach the men's quarters with, in front of you on the right, the big courtyard of the *palaestra* with its surrounding porticos. A number of rooms lead off to the left. To the left of the first room (the undressing room) is the men's *frigidarium* with its circular bath. Leading out of the undressing room you come to the *tepidarium* and then the *caldarium*. The entrance to the women's quarters is in *Cardo* IV, No. 8, with a similar series of rooms but on a smaller, more intimate scale; these are better preserved and have a fine mosaic with a Triton.

(4) *The Casa con due atrii* has two stories. The inner atrium had sleeping-quarters above it. At the end of *Cardo* III, adjoining the *Decumanus maximus*, the big *Collegio dei Augustales* has now been excavated and restored. It is an impressive hall in which the priests of the imperial cult had their meetings. The painted apse at the end was dedicated to Hercules.

CARDO IV

(5) *Casa del Bel Cortile* (No. 8). This has an unusual plan with step leading to the upper floor from a little raised courtyard. The mosaic and painted decoration is delightful, and on the ground floor you can see a collection of some of the objects found in the excavations, including a marble statue of young Eros, as well as portraits of some of the well-known citizens etc.

(6) *The Casa del mosaico di Nettuno e Anfitrite* (No. 7) is on two floors and has a wine shop beside it. This is the best-preserved house in Herculaneum or Pompeii. A big richly decorated atrium with mosaics of hunting scenes etc. The shop still has its wares displayed for sale. (See Plate 4.)

(7) *Casa del mobilio carbonizzato* (No. 5) is a small pre-Roman house decorated in the Claudian period. One room has a picture of Pan discovering a sleeping nymph. Further in is a room with windows looking out onto a courtyard. This house still contains some carbonized furniture and a bed. It is interesting to note the stylistic origins of our own late 18th- and early 19th-century furniture.

At the angle of the *Cardo* IV with the *Decumanus inferiore* is the

(8) *Casa Sannitica*, with the entrance to the women's baths almost opposite. This house (No. 1) is one of the earliest at Herculaneum, and as the name suggests it is an Italic rather than a Roman type of house. Its entrance is fine, and note specially the atrium with, on the first floor, a loggia with small Ionic columns. The decoration of the first room is in the First style (see p. 58), with imitation polychrome marble.

(9) *The Casa del tramezzo di legno* (Nos. 11 and 12) has a fine façade of two floors, quite unusually well preserved. Decorated with mosaics and frescoes, two of the small bedrooms still contain their beds. The most interesting feature of the house is its three-doored screen of carbonized wood. There is a delightful small garden surrounded by a

portico supported on pilasters, with rest rooms below it. It is interesting
to find that the central one of these rooms has a painting showing a view
of the garden.

(**10**) *Casa a graticcio* (Nos. 13–17) is the only complete artisan-type
house. It is made with wattle-and-daub construction.

(**11**) *Casa del atrio a mosaico* (Nos. 1 and 2). A fine house decorated with
frescoes and mosaics. Some rooms have windows still retaining their
wooden framing. A marble vase stands in the centre of the garden.
A large triclinium is flanked by small decorated rooms, and the house
has a covered loggia and an open terrace once overlooking the sea.

On the opposite side of the road at No. 19 is all that remains of the
so-called (**12**) *Casa dell'Albergo*, now, owing to bad excavations in the
past, all that is left of one of the most splendid houses in the southern
part of the town. In the *Decumanus inferiore* (No. 35) is the *Casa del
grande portale* with its fine entrance flanked by half-columns with
Corinthian capitals. The main room is decorated with paintings.

DECUMANO MASSIMO

(**13**) **Casa del Bicentenario* (Nos. 15–16). Huge square atrium. Fine
painted and marble decorated rooms, one with a folding wooden lattice
door. The rooms on the upper floor are simple, but one is particularly
interesting for it has what seems to be the imprint of a wooden cross in a
stucco panel, and if this is so it is very early evidence for the diffusion
of Christianity, since, as we know, the town was wiped out in A.D. 79.
St. Paul had visited the area in 61.

CARDO V

(**14**) *Casa del Atrio Corinzio* (No. 30) is a charming house with a small
porch. There are a number of household objects displayed here.
(Opposite it at No. 10 is a small shop with a bed, and at No. 8 another
shop with its oven for bread and pastry making.)

(**15**) *Casa del Sacello di legno* (No. 31) was decorated in the republican
period. The house is remarkable for a curious wooden altar in the form
of a little temple to the household gods: it stands in an alcoved room on
the right of the entrance, and has cupboards below. Nearly opposite,
and in line with the *Decumanus Inferiore*, is the entrance sloping down
to the *palaestra* (gymnasium), still only partially excavated. A trial
excavation cut into the deposits still covering the central area has

revealed the bronze fountain which stood there: an unattractive but ingenious design with waterspouts in the form of snakes' heads.

A Pistrinum with a corn-grinding mill and oven is at No. 1.

(**16**) *★Casa del Relievo di Telefo* (Nos. 2 and 3) is a very big house with decorations mostly belonging to the latest phase. It has richly decorated rooms and a colonnaded garden. Fine marble decorations in one room, and in a small room leading off it is a relief of Telephus, a son of Hercules. This is neo-Attic art of the I century B.C.

(**17**) *★Casa dei Cervi* (No. 5) is one of the richest houses in the town. It covers a huge rectangular area with the northern quarters around the entrance and the southern ones with terraces overlooking the sea. One of the rooms contains a pair of magnificently sculptured groups with dogs attacking deer, originally in the garden. Another room has a statuette of a satyr with a wineskin (a variant of a bronze one from Pompeii). There is a loggia and a pergola, with its original flower vases on pilasters. Another room contains a statuette of Hercules who has had too much to drink.

(**18**) *Casa della Gemma* (No. 1) called after a Claudian gem found here. It has a richly decorated atrium. See the kitchen with pots still on the hearth.

Beyond these last two houses was the Porta Marina or sea-gate.

Outside the main excavated area are several other important buildings including the once best-preserved bath buildings known, (**19**) the *Terme suburbane*. These have unavoidably suffered in recent years.

The Theatre can sometimes be visited at No. 119 of Corso Ercolano. It is only of interest to specialists, having been largely ransacked by its 18th-century discoverers. It is of Augustan and later date.

The Villa dei Papiri cannot be visited. A very splendid house, it was unfortunately found, too early for scientific excavation, in the 18th century, and contained wonderfully rich sculptural bronzes (*Museo Nazionale*), and a whole library of papyrus rolls, mostly of Epicurean writings, now in the *Biblioteca Nazionale* in the Palazzo Reale, Naples.

Ischia (Greek *Pithekoussai*)

This beautiful island was formed, like the Phlegraean Fields, under volcanic conditions which gave rise to the mineral springs and other natural thermal qualities for which it is now famous.

It has suffered from a number of eruptions during its history which began long before the Greeks colonized it: contacts had already been made with the eastern Mediterranean at least as early as 1400 B.C., for Mycenaean III C sherds have been discovered both in Ischia itself and in the nearby island of Vivara.

Livy wrote that Pithekoussai had been founded by the Euboeans before they founded Cumae, and this may well be true for late Geometric and Protocorinthian pottery has been found in tombs on the Monte di Vico promontory, and San Montano has produced an early VIII century Syrian seal and other finds witnessing trade activities at a very early date with Greece and the Aegean, Syria and Egypt, as well as with the Etruscans and local Italic peoples.

The Euboeans from Eretria and Chalcis, who had probably founded the colony to facilitate the trading of Etruscan metals with the Greek world, were, according to Pliny and Strabo, forced to abandon Ischia after a violent eruption at the end of the VI century. In 474 B.C., after Hieron I of Syracuse had defeated the Etruscans in the sea battle off Cumae, he occupied the island and then left troops there, but they remained only four years before they were driven out by another violent eruption. Nevertheless in Roman times, from the late IV century onwards, and particularly at the time of Augustus, the island was a favoured place for retirement.

Today there are few remains of antiquity. The *Museum* near the harbour at 125 Via Roma (open Sundays from 10.30 to 12.30 and Thursdays from 4.30 to 6.30) contains local finds. At *Lacco Ameno*, under the church of Santa Restituta, there are remains of an early Christian church of the 4th–5th century.

Lake Avernus (see Fig. 6)

This is visible from the road above, near the *Arco Felice* (p. 34), but can best be approached from the south, from a turning off the Baia–Pozzuoli road. In ancient times thickly wooded slopes dropped down to the still, dark waters of the lake, formed in a volcanic crater, and the awe-inspiring character of the place, helped no doubt by its gaseous vapours, gave rise to the belief that it was the entrance into the Infernal Regions (see p. 31). Many legends grew up, many poets described it, and many famous men, including Hannibal, offered sacrifices to Pluto, god of the underworld. In 37 B.C., however, the less superstitious and far more practical Romans radically altered the character of the lake, at the time of the civil war between Antony and Octavian, when Agrippa, acting for Octavian, had all the trees felled and cut a canal from the south bank of the lake to link it with Lake Lucrino and the sea, and from the opposite bank an underground gallery (the *Grotta di Cocceio*, see below) leading towards Cumae. In this way the lake was transformed into the famous but short-lived military harbour and dockyard known as the *Portus Julius*. Volcanic alterations, however, soon led to the obstruction of the canal, and the harbour was abandoned.

The surrounding area grew popular in imperial Roman times and was dotted with villas and temples, and a huge bath-building complex stood on the east bank. Called the '*Temple of Apollo*', this had a vast cupola, only very little smaller than that of the Pantheon, and was probably built during the reign of Hadrian, or slightly later.

The Grotta di Cocceio (now no longer open to the public) was once entered from near the *Arco Felice*. This underground gallery (see above) was a remarkable engineering feat, carried out in about 38 B.C. and named after its probable designer Lucius Cocceius, working on a plan for Octavian's admiral Agrippa, to improve the port facilities at Cumae. This tunnel was to pass from the level of Lake Avernus to Cumae, while another was to pass under the acropolis to the beach, and in this way convoys could avoid passing round the Cape Misenum.

Literno (Roman *Liternum*)

Some remains of the Roman town can be visited, 12 km. to the north of Cumae, on the coast. The excavated buildings, which are not particularly spectacular, include the foundations of an Italic-type temple of the II B.C., a forum, and a rather later basilica and theatre. The Forum has an altar engraved with a couplet written by Ennius to record the burial of Scipio Africanus, conqueror of Hannibal who, as we know from Seneca, retired here, disgusted by the accusations made against him by an ungrateful country, to live in simple retirement till he died in 183 B.C. Livy wrote, 'Scipio lived out his life in Liternum and had no longing for the capital. On his deathbed, they say, he gave orders that he was to be buried in his rural retreat, and that his tomb was to be erected there.'

Much of the town lies under the sand-dunes. Though mentioned by Cicero and other writers, it never played an important rôle in history.

NAPLES

Museo Archeologico Nazionale (Piazza Museo Nazionale)

Opening hours 9.30–4; holidays, 9.30–1.30. See Figs. 8, 9 and 10.
This is one of the richest collections of antiquities in the world. As at

the time of going to press there are no guide-books available in English, and as the objects are mostly only marked with a number, an attempt has been made here, within the available limit of space, to draw attention to at least the more interesting objects displayed. The arrangement of the collections is as follows:

GROUND FLOOR	Large marbles	Entrance Hall
	Archaic sculptures	Room I
	Classical Greek sculptures and Roman Copies	Rooms II–XVI and XXIV–XXVIII
	Prehistory (small collection) and Egyptology	Rooms XVII–XXIII
	Painted marbles of divinities etc.	Room XXIX
	Bronze statues and portrait busts from Herculaneum and elsewhere	Rooms XXX and XL–XLV
	Epigraphy	Room XLVI

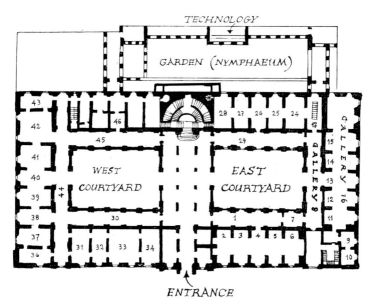

Fig. 8 Naples. Museo Nazionale. Plan of Ground Floor.

COURTYARD	Early technology and mechanics	(See also Room XCV on the First Floor)
MEZZANINE (*Ammezzato*)	Mosaics	Rooms LVII–LXI
FIRST FLOOR	Large bronzes (Herculaneum and Pompeii)	Rooms off the *Grande Salone dell'Atlante*
	Wall-Paintings	Rooms LXVI–LXXVIII
	Armour and weapons	Room LXXIX
	Ivories and glazed terracottas	Room LXXX
	Coloured glass	Room LXXXI
	Silver	Room LXXXII
	Gold jewellery etc.	Room LXXXIII
	Glass	Room LXXXIV
	Small bronzes (shortly to be put next to the large bronzes)	
	Lighting and heating in Pompeii and Herculaneum	Room XCIV
	Technology	Room XCV (see also Courtyard off Ground Floor)
	Scale model of Pompeii	Room XCVI
	Terracottas	Room LXXXVI (architectural) Room LXXXVII (figurines) Room LXXXVIII (large statues)
SECOND FLOOR	*Pottery*	
	Cumae	Room XCVII
	Italic and Etruscan	Room XCVIII
	Early Attic	Room XCIX
	Later Attic	Room C
	Apulian, Lucanian and Campanian	Rooms CI–CV

TECHNOLOGICAL COLLECTION

In the courtyard there is an important collection of ancient technology

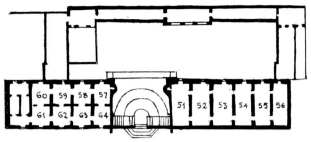

Fig. 9 Naples. Museo Nazionale. Plan of Mezzanine.

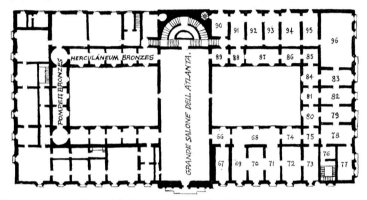

Fig. 10 Naples. Museo Nazionale. Plan of First Floor.

and mechanics, the only one of its kind in Europe. In the central garden is a reproduction of (1/10) a sea-water swimming pool from a Roman villa at Formiae. The sculpture under the portico came from Baiae. The collections comprise authentic instruments and apparatus only the wooden parts of which are modern reproductions. Some large equipment remaining on the sites of Pompeii and Herculaneum is here reproduced on a smaller scale. Various machines for the mechanical working of grain and bread, for pressing grapes, extracting oil from olives, weights and measures, sundials, astrological spheres, architectural instruments etc. There is also the imprint in limestone concretion of a hydraulic wheel as described by Vitruvius.

(Note that surgical, optical and other smaller instruments are displayed in Room XCV on the First Floor.)

ENTRANCE HALL **Large sarcophagi and Imperial Roman sculptures**

Some from Herculaneum are portraits of the family of Marcus Nonius

Balbus. **6167**, Balbus himself, a statue set up by decree in Herculaneum; **5993**, huge statue of Alexander Severus; **6122** *and* **6116**, statues of Dacian prisoners with their characteristic Phrygian caps etc.; **1793**, base of a commemorative monument from Pozzuoli. (This is a smaller version of one set up to record the rebuilding by Tiberius of towns destroyed by earthquakes in Asia Minor in A.D. 17 and 30.) Around the base of the monument were 14 statues personifying the rebuilt towns. According to an inscription this version from Pozzuoli was dedicated by the priests of Augustus in A.D. 30. **6233**, statue of Marcus Olconius Rufus, one of the city magistrates in Pompeii; **6705**, sarcophagus from Pozzuoli, representing the creation and destruction of Man (3rd century A.D.).

Room I. **Archaic sculptures**
6556, Vth century funerary stele in Greek marble; **6009** and **6010**, Harmodius and Aristogeiton who slew Hipparchus in 514 B.C. A good Roman copy of a bronze group made in 477 B.C. **6006**, group of two statues said to represent Orestes and Electra, from the market place (so-called Temple of Serapis) at Pozzuoli. The two original elements are of different age and origin, worked into a composition at the very end of republican times.

Rooms II–XVI. **Mostly V century Greek sculpture and Roman copies** (see also Rooms XXIV–XXVIII).

Room II. **5998** and **5997**, 2 statues of Aphrodite; **6005**, large head of Artemis, or more probably Kore, copy of V century original; **6024**, statue, possibly Athena, a good imperial Roman copy of a figure dedicated by Pericles, and set up on the Acropolis in 430 B.C.; **6727**, relief of Orpheus, Eurydice and Hermes. This belongs to a large series of similar reliefs, very like one from the Parthenon frieze, and the original one may have come from the Altar of Pity in the Agora at Athens: **6322**, Athena with Attic helmet, probably 450–425 B.C. *Room III*. **6269**, V century goddess; **6011**, an interesting statue found at Pompeii, this is the best known copy of Polycleitus's masterpiece of an athlete with a spear, made originally in bronze in about 450 B.C. and for long regarded as the ideal for manly proportions.

Room IV. **144978**, statue of Diomedes from Cumae, a copy of a mid-V century original attributed to Kresilas and signed by the Roman copyist.

Rooms V and VI contained a few finds from early excavations at Greek towns in Southern Italy. By the time this book is published they may have been restored to the local museums in their places of origin. **145070** *and* **145080**, decorative Nereids from a swimming pool at Formiae: inspired by IV–III century Hellenistic art, they were probably made somewhere in Magna Graecia; **131209**, enormous statue of a Dioscurus from Baiae.

Room VII. **119917**, imperial Roman copy of a statue of a victorious young athlete, the bronze original of which probably belonged to the V century B.C.

Gallery VIII. In centre **5999**, huge group from the Baths of Caracalla in Rome: its subject is under discussion, and the original version was Hellenistic; **6409**, huge female figure, perhaps Aphrodite, from the Baths of Caracalla (2nd–3rd century copy of IV century B.C. original); **6301**, Venus and a dolphin: copy of IV century B.C. work; **6276**, Artemis the huntress: inspired from Attic work of IV century B.C.

Room IX (Amazons and Warriors). **6014, 6013, 6015, 6012** and **6405**. This is a very important and impressive collection, almost all of it belonging to one large composition. Two copies of this now exist, and these present figures probably came from the version made for the Acropolis. Attalus I, King of Pergamon, had 4 groups of figures made to commemorate his victories over the Gauls who had invaded Asia Minor in 239 B.C. The complete sculpture represented the victory of Greek civilization over the barbarians, gods over giants, Athenians over the Amazons, Athenians over Persians, Attalus over the Gauls.

Room X. **6020**, statue of Venus Callipygos: a fine Roman copy of a Hellenistic original. Several other Roman copies of Hellenistic Venuses, and **6289**, from the Temple of Isis at Pompeii.

Room XI. **124325**, tomb from Atella with a relief of Achilles with the daughters of Lycomedes (2nd century); **6726**, fine Neo-Attic style Bacchic procession.

Room XII. The Farnese Hercules (like many other marble statues in the museum, once belonging to the Farnese collection in Rome) is a huge statue found in the Baths of Caracalla in Rome: this is an Athenian copy of a bronze original by Lysippus. On wall, copy of IV century B.C. original of male torso; **6035**, magnificent torso of Aphrodite, thought by some to be by Praxiteles.

Room XIII. **6260**, left of passage, enormous mask of Jupiter, copy of well-known IV century B.C. Greek original; **6682**, the seduction of Helen, a good copy of original IV century B.C. Attic relief showing Paris meeting Helen and Aphrodite.

Room XIV. **6019**, Psyche, Venus or Andromeda freed by Perseus; this with **6017** (Aphrodite, or the 'Venus of Capua') came from the amphitheatre at Santa Maria Capua Vetere.

Room XV. Various statues of Dionysus and satyrs, and **6329**, a repro-duction of a famous Hellenistic work with Pan giving a music lesson.

Gallery XVI (Galleria del Toro Farnese). Centre, **6002**, the great group known as the Farnese Bull, from the Baths of Caracalla. It shows the revenge of Zethos and Amphion on Dirce, Queen of Thebes. The original of this group was carried out in bronze by two Hellenistic sculptors from Asia Minor, and Pliny described it as an admirable piece of work. This is a much patched-up copy of the 2nd or 3rd century.

Prehistory and Egyptology

(Rooms XVII–XXIII. Not always open, and some of the antiquities from here are now being restored to their place of origin in local Italian museums, so they are not described here.)

Rooms XXIV–XXVII. **Decorative sculptures and reliefs,** mostly showing hunting scenes etc. Note **110565**, in the last room, with a scene of fighting ships.

Room XXIX. Passage with painted marbles, mostly of deities. **9372** and **9370**, Isis; **6262**, Apollo, black basalt Roman copy of Hellenistic original; **6723** and **6764**, reliefs of Mithras sacrificing the bull (for this god see pages 81–82); **6371**, the oriental goddess Cybele; **6278** (at side of passage room), Artemis of Ephesus, with hands, feet and face in bronze, (imperial Roman copy of the statue worshipped in the Sanctuary at Ephesus, the four rows of breasts symbolizing the goddess's power to bestow fertility); **981**, the Egyptian god Anubis. Also note, on the walls, some votive reliefs from Ischia with Apollo and the Nymphs, guardians of the mineral waters.

Room XXX. Galleria di Ercolano. Bronze statue portraits of citizens of Herculaneum, many of Claudian date. **5593** is a heroic statue of the Emperor Claudius himself, and others may be members of his family; **5615** portrays Tiberius clothed for sacrificing; **115390** is a horse's head from one of the six gilded equestrian statues once decorating the theatre at Herculaneum; **4904**, in centre, represents one horse from part of a magnificent quadriga (4-horsed chariot).

(*Rooms XXXI–XXXV.* Recently subject to alteration and re-numbering.)

Room XXXVI. In centre the well-known large horse's head, at one time thought to have been by Donatello but now considered to be ancient, perhaps III century B.C. Around the walls are bronze fragments from the 4-horsed chariot at Herculaneum. Pass through the next two rooms to *Room XXXIX* where **6068** is a huge bust of Vespasian.

Room XL. **6038**, huge bust of Julius Caesar. In the centre is a fine portrait of Augustus.

Room XLI. Large statue of Tiberius (**6000** and **6051**); **110892**, Titus.

Room XLII. A number of portrait busts and statues, many of emperors. Numbers **6763, 6753, 6757, 6739, 6738** are decorative elements from the grandiose building (*Poseidonium*) once in the Piazza di Pietra in Rome. This, a Corinthian temple, was restored by Hadrian and embellished by the Antonines. It personified the various provinces in the Empire.

Room XLIII. Roman portraits. Note **6086**, Septimius Severus. Pass through the next room to:

Room XLIV. Galleria degli Imperatori. Mostly statues of Roman Emperors. **5617**, Tiberius; **5635**, in centre, Claudius on horseback; **6059**, Titus; **6092**, Marcus Aurelius; **6033**, Caracalla; **6056**, huge seated figure of Tiberius; **6075**, Hadrian; **6031**, Antoninus Pius; etc.

Room XLV. Gallery of Greek portraits. **6239,** Herodotus and Thucydides portrayed together; **6160,** Euripides; **6129,** Socrates; **6150,** Pyrrhus. Behind **6126** (Homer?) a door leads to *Room XLVI.* This is the **Epigraphical collection** with topographically arranged inscriptions.

MEZZANINE OR AMMEZZATO (in course of rearrangement) **Mosaics**

(Note that the paintings from Pompeii and Herculaneum now in Rooms LI–LVI are to be transferred to the First Floor.)

Rooms LVII–LXIV contain the mosaics, almost all of which come from Pompeii and form the richest collection in existence. The earliest mosaics were simply made, first with black and white pebbles, then with square terracotta tesserae, then the use of coloured stones became common, and finally the rich variety of coloured tesserae which, particularly when made by Alexandrian mosaicists, reach unparalleled perfection and quality. Most of the houses in Pompeii and Herculaneum were built or embellished at the moment of greatest artistic achievement, but just before they were destroyed a new vogue was coming into fashion— floors made with inlaid marbles from Egypt etc.

Many of the scenes shown in these mosaics are easy to interpret. One or two of special interest are: *Room LVII.* **10016,** Theseus and the Minotaur; **109678,** Venus.

Room LVIII. **109982,** and **9978,** skull and skeleton (the sight of these during banquets was intended to spur you to enjoy life while you could). *Room LIX.* **9987,** a young woman accompanied by an older one is trying to persuade a sorceress to give her a love philtre—evidently a scene from a play. This is signed by the mosaicist Dioscurides of Samos. **9985,** wandering minstrels, by the same artist; **124545,** an interesting scene with a philosopher (Plato?) teaching with a sphere: possibly the Acropolis in the background; **124666,** fine female portrait in minute tesserae; **120177,** lively mosaic with marine fauna and a lobster fighting an octopus.

Room LX. **9993,** cat biting a quail, with beautifully observed birds and animals below.

Room LXI. **10020,** the famous picture-like mosaic of the *Battle between Darius and Alexander* found in the Casa del Fauno in Pompeii. This must be a copy of a big composition depicting, in all probability, the battle of Issos between the Persians and Macedonians under their respective kings. It must have been made in Alexandria, transported in sections, and laid in Pompeii.

FIRST FLOOR (partly in course of rearrangement)

Grande Salone dell' Atlante called after the famous Hellenistic statue of Atlas.

The rooms off to the right now house the **Large bronzes from Pompeii and Herculaneum,** the richest collection in the world. Once these decorative or commemorative bronzes stood in private houses or gardens or in public buildings until they were buried and preserved under the volcanic ash and slime from the eruption of Vesuvius in A.D. 79. A great many came from the Villa dei Papiri, one of the most sumptuous villas known. Many are excellent Roman copies of Greek works of art, often now lost, and they therefore have a double importance. It is impossible to list these individually, but those perhaps most worth noting are: **5625,** Hermes, probably from an original by Lysippus; **5624,** sleeping satyr; **48886** and **4888,** two figures of deer; **5634,** portrait of Scipio Africanus, conqueror of Hannibal; **5616,** head of an old man (perhaps Seneca); **143753,** one of the most prized bronzes in the museum, which is the statue of a young man, or Ephebe, making a votive offering: an excellent copy of a V century B.C. original; **5630,** Apollo, after an original perhaps by Hegias, master of Phidias: he must once have held a musical instrument, as he holds a plectrum; **4994,** Alexander the Great or one of his cavalrymen in battle: copy of Lysippus school. **136683,** Heracles: this is a large copy of a work by Lysippus made as a trophy for Alexander the Great; **110663,** Lucius Caecilius Jocundus—a particularly interesting bronze as it represents one of the most notable citizens of Pompeii, in whose house were found a whole archive of waxed tablets which have shed much light on the subject of Roman private rights.

111495, satyr with a wineskin from the Casa del Centenario at Pompeii; **5003,** Narcissus: its rather heavy treatment suggests that the original came from the school of Praxiteles; **4997,** Victory (certain elements such as the sphere are not original); **5002,** Dancing Faun, once in the centre of the atrium of the Casa del Fauno at Pompeii: copy of a Hellenistic original.

In the centre of the last room in the series devoted to Large Bronzes is the remarkable decorated tripod from the Temple of Isis at Pompeii.

Rooms LXVI–LXXVIII on the other side of the Grande Salone dell'
Atlante. **Wall-Paintings.**

These come from Herculaneum, Pompeii and Stabiae which were
all destroyed or damaged in the eruption of Vesuvius in A.D. 79, and they
belong to the I century B.C.–1st A.D. A separate collection includes some
from Lucanian, Apulian and Campanian tombs, though these are less fine
than the wonderful series recently discovered at Paestum (see pp. 202–
203).

The Pompeian and contemporary styles of wall-painting are nowadays
divided stylistically and chronologically into several styles, as follows:
First (or Incrustation) *style.* This goes back to the III–II century B.C.
when the walls were painted to imitate marble slabs.
Second style. I century B.C. With increasing wealth the decoration
became more lavish and landscape painting was specially popular. The
painters were often Greeks brought up from the Hellenized south. A
fine example of this style is the big frieze of the triclinium in the Villa
dei Misteri not far from the Porta Ercolanese at Pompeii, and another,
which came from the Villa of Fannius Sinister at Boscoreale near
Pompeii, is now in Naples Museum (Room LXIX).
Third style (so-called 'Ornate') is much more fanciful and is permeated
with Egyptian influence. It developed in the late I century B.C. A typical
example is in the house of Lucretius Fronto at Pompeii.
Fourth style. End of Augustan period till A.D. 79. Often shows stage
scenery and sometimes a play in progress, as for instance in the house
of Pinarius Cerialis in Pompeii in which one room opens to show a stage
with the *Iphigenia in Tauris* being acted. Vitruvius described scene
paintings from the Hellenistic East, and these may have had an influence.
The remaining style at Pompeii is known as the *Intricate style.* The whole
of the wall surface was plastered in white and then painted with a lattice-
work of various designs which were then waxed to make them brilliant.
A good example is in the house of the Vettii. This style was frequently
used in the *columbarium* tombs of the I century B.C. and later, and is
sometimes called by that name.

There are far too many paintings to allow more than a few of outstanding beauty or interest to be noted.

Room LXVII. **9351, 9363, 9364,** paintings from a Paestan tomb with
Samnite warriors and cavalry. *Room LXVIII.* Note the curious baroque
architecture of number **9731.** *Room LXIX.* Theatrical scene, perhaps
from *Antigone*, set in the Hellenistic period, from a villa at Boscoreale

outside Pompeii. *Room LXX.* **9111**, *Iphigenia in Tauris. Room LXXI.* In two parts, near the window, a big composition from Herculaneum: on the right Hercules is watching his son Telephus being suckled by a deer; **9049**, Theseus and the Minotaur etc. *Room LXXII.* **9559**, Marriage of Zeus, after an unknown IV century B.C. Greek painter; **8998**, Perseus and Andromeda, after the original by the IV century B.C. Athenian Nicias; **8976**, part of a fine painting of Medea about to kill her children who are playing knucklebones with their teacher. In the centre of this room there are unique examples of paintings on marble. **9562**, neo-Attic in style, and bearing the artist's signature, shows various mythical characters playing games. **9043**, Theseus receiving thanks after having killed the Minotaur.

Room LXXIII. **111436**, Jason and Pelias. In this story the usurper of Jason's kingdom was warned by the oracle against a man wearing only one sandal. Here Jason (bottom right) has terrified Pelias and his sons who are making a sacrifice to Poseidon; **111474**, Hercules, Deianira and Nessus. There are many other legendary subjects in the next two rooms. *Room LXXV* contains a painting depicting three scenes referring to the origins of Rome, the lower scene showing Romulus and Remus with the wolf. This is interesting as it is earlier than the many sculptural works dedicated to the subject. *Room LXXVII.* Mostly scenes with countryside and villas; **9514**, the harbour of a local town, perhaps Pozzuoli; **112222**, the fight between men of Pompeii and Nocera which, according to Tacitus, took place in the amphitheatre at Pompeii in A.D. 59. In this informative scene you can see the amphitheatre with the temporary booths and tents of refreshment sellers etc. and the big *velarium* or awning which is haif drawn back to show the fighting. **8924**: before a Temple of Isis a priest is showing people the sacred urn containing water from the Nile; **9069**: itinerant vendors in the Forum at Pompeii. *Room LXXVIII.* **9423**, unusual painting of trees and architecture.

Collection of Precious objects

Room LXXIX. Armour and weapons. Many of these are from Pompeii and include some fine gladiatorial parade armour and weapons used for the march-past before the combats. There are also weapons from Lucanian and Samnite towns; **5673**, gladiator's helmet with scenes showing Helen and Menelaus, Ajax and Cassandra etc.; **5674**, helmet showing the apotheosis of Rome.

Room LXXX. Ivories and glazed terracottas. Fine collection of bone and ivory objects, nearly all from Pompeii. The glazed terracottas were imported from Alexandria.

Room LXXXI. Coloured glass and crystal. Mostly from Pompeii. Note particularly the masterly blue glass vase, **13521**, from a tomb belonging to the Villa delle Colonne in Pompeii. The bright blue glass was first painted with white vitreous paste and the figures then cut back to expose the underlying colour.

Room LXXXII. Silver. In the centre a table service of over 100 pieces from the Casa del Menandro in Pompeii. Another magnificent service is in a wall case and came from the house called the Casa dell' Argenteria.

Room LXXXIII. Gold jewellery, etc. Divided into two sections with the earlier pieces (VIII to VI century B.C. from Cumae and Etruria) to the Hellenistic period (III and II century B.C.) near the window. The rest of the collection is Roman and almost all came from Pompeii. In the centre is the prize piece **27611**, the so-called Farnese cup made at the end of the time of the Ptolemies, in the late I century B.C. of brown and grey streaked sardonyx. On the outside is a large head of a Gorgon, while on the inside the scenes show the glorification of the annual flooding of the Nile, with Isis in the lower part. In the middle Horus is holding a ploughshare in his left hand and his right hand rests on a yoked plough-handle. Two winged figures represent the winds and are busily blowing to stop the flowing of the Nile and so cause it to flood. On the lower right, two seated Nymphs may personify the two main seasons in Egypt, the seasons of flooding and harvesting. On the left the Nile, with a large cornucopia. This piece was certainly made in Alexandria.

Room LXXXIV. Household glass, etc. Glass in daily use and some more important pieces demonstrating the techniques by which they were made.

Room LXXXV. Large cinerary urns, plates, bottles etc.

The Collection of Terracottas

These are displayed in three rooms according to subject: architectural terracottas, figurines and large statues.

Room LXXXVI. Various architectural fragments mostly from temples in Magna Graecia. These may soon be sent back to the museums now being built in the localities from which they came.

Room LXXXVII. Votive terracottas from different parts of Campania and the towns of Magna Graecia.

Room LXXXVIII. Big terracotta statues.

Room LXXXIX. Small marble statues.

The Collection of Small Bronzes (Figurines, vases, etc.). These are about to be removed from their present rooms (*XC–XCIII*) and will be put next to the large bronzes. Although most of these small bronzes came from Herculaneum and Pompeii, there are also some Etruscan mirrors and a rich collection of Italic (non-Greek) bronzes.

Room XCIV. **Lighting and heating of Pompeian and Herculanean houses.**

Room XCV. **Technology**, weights, measures, surveying instruments, musical instruments, bronze furniture fittings, surgical (perhaps veterinary) and optical instruments including the only known example of a *speculum uteri* etc. (Note that the mechanical and larger technological equipment is in a separate building in the North Courtyard.)

Room XCVI. Large model of Pompeii (scale 1/100) in the centre of the room, and around the walls paintings of gardens and still-life, showing a remarkable observation of natural detail. In one case there are carbonized remains of figs, nuts, grain, eggs, bread etc. Some reconstructed furniture is also displayed, with the original bronze fittings. Bronze vases and candelabra.

On the balcony above there are faithful reproductions in water-colour of Pompeian mosaics and wall-paintings.

SECOND FLOOR (**Pottery**)

Room XCVII. Collection of finds from the Cumae necropolis, some of
the VII century. The earliest pottery is followed by two groups: on the
right wall imported red- and black-figure Attic vases, and on the left
wall Italiot vases (made in various centres in Magna Graecia). Many of
these are decorated with battle scenes, or with events in the afterworld,
and they make much use of superimposed yellows, greens and reds.

Room XCVIII. Italic and Etruscan pottery, mostly VII–VI century B.C.
and often imitating wares imported from the eastern Mediterranean.
The Italic wares come from Apulia, Campania etc., and the Etruscan
pottery includes VII century B.C. bucchero ware which was also copied
by the indigenous peoples.

Rooms XCIX and C. Attic and Corinthian pottery. Important imported
wares which often include vases painted by well-known painters. The
first room contains the earlier pottery, Protocorinthian, Corinthian,
much black-figure and red-figure ware. The next room, *C*, has mostly
V–IV century B.C. Attic pottery. Experts will be able to recognize many
of the legendary and mythical figures represented. **2492** is a fine red-
figure hydria showing the night of the destruction of Troy, with the
aged Priam about to be killed by Ajax.

The next four or five rooms are dedicated to wares produced in Italy
under Greek influence or by Greek craftsmen settled there. Each district
has its own distinctive character.

Room CI. Apulian wares from Ruvo di Puglia, mostly with legendary
and mythological scenes.

Room CII. Canosan wares (from Canosa di Puglia). Another type of
Apulian ware, some of it richly coloured and very baroque in form and
reminding one of the Hellenistic pottery produced at Centuripe in
Sicily. The great masterpiece here, made somewhere in Apulia, is **3253,**
the so-called 'Darius Vase' with three registers of decoration lauding the
struggle between Greece and the East. The upper register shows Zeus
receiving Hellas brought by Athena; in the central register Darius
enthroned listens to the debate between councillors and delegates from
the province (shortly before the battle of Marathon in 480 B.C. won by
the Greeks); the third shows Bellerophon and the Chimera.

Room CIII. Lucanian and Paestan wares made at various centres, from the V century when their production began, until the Roman conquest of Lucania in the early III century B.C. Some of the Paestan vases are signed by Assteas. **2873**, Aryballos with Hercules in the garden of the Hesperides, etc.

Room CIV. Campanian wares of IV–III century B.C. Most of these come from a workshop at ancient *Saticulum* (S. Agata dei Goti), and others are from Cumae, Abella and minor places.

Room CV. In course of rearrangement.

Nocera Inferiore (ancient *Nuceria Alfaterna*, and Roman *Nuceria Constantia*)

Originally possibly an indigenous town, it was taken over by a succession of settlers, first Etruscans, then Samnites (in the V century B.C.) and finally by the Romans in 307 B.C. It was destroyed by Hannibal in 216, sacked first by the Romans and then by Spartacus, and eventually made a colony called *Nuceria Constantia*.

Between Nocera Inferiore and Superiore there are some unspectacular remains of Roman date. Some interesting local antiquities, including a rich collection of vases painted in the Paestan and Campanian styles, can be seen in the *Museo dell' Agro Nocerino* in the Convent of Sant' Antonio.

Near Nocera Superiore is the important 5th century building, originally a baptistery, of Santa Maria Maggiore (or della Rotonda). It has been restored many times, but still retains much of interest and a remarkable sculptured font.

Nola

In the Seminario built by Vanvitelli there are some Roman inscriptions, and one of the most important inscriptions we have in the Oscan language. This was found at *Abella* (now Avella), and it refers to a treaty made in the mid-II century B.C. Ask in the Biblioteca for the *Cippus abellanus*.

Near to Nola is Cimitile which was a prosperous Samnite and then Roman centre in antiquity, trading in grain and wine. There are a number of Early-Christian remains, both architectural and sculptural, in the Basilica di San Felix.

Pompeii

Pompeii today, because of its exceptional state of preservation, is perhaps the most visited site of antiquity in Europe, but unless you are a specialized student of Roman life, and particularly if your time in the district is limited, the best way to obtain an idea of how the Romans lived is to make only a selective visit to Pompeii, including, of course, the Villa dei Misteri, outside the town near the Porto Ercolano, and then to spend time in the *Museo Archeologico* in Naples (which houses so many of the fine mosaics and paintings, small and large bronzes and other finds from the excavations), and the small, equally well-preserved but more intimate and more patrician town of Herculaneum. A selective plan of Pompeii can be seen in Fig. 11, in which the more important houses and public buildings have been indicated. The ideal time for visiting, to avoid the crowds, is on summer evenings from 8 to 11 p.m. (for details of visiting hours and transport to the site, see below).

Pompeii was a thriving residential and commercial town of about 20,000 inhabitants when it was overwhelmed by the disastrous eruption of Vesuvius on August 24th, A.D. 79, which buried the town under a thick layer of burning ashes and cinders. The most distinguished man to lose his life on this occasion was the elder Pliny who was commanding the fleet at Cape Misenum, sent to help in the rescue operations. The whole disaster, including the death of his uncle, has been vividly described by the younger Pliny in a letter to Tacitus (*Book VI*. no. 20). Before this Pompeii had a long and, like all ancient towns, chequered history about which something must be related before passing to the description of some of the more important buildings.

The town, which stood about a mile from the sea, and which had a small harbour at the mouth of the river Sarno, was founded by Italic peoples, attracted by the rich land around, and the straggling, haphazard layout of the streets in the south-west corner belongs to this phase. These people were soon afterwards joined by Greeks who set up a colony at about the same time as they founded the nearby settlement of Cumae. They were particularly influential in the religious life of the community, and both the earlier temple (? VI century B.C.) and the VI century temple of Apollo are Greek in form; moreover Greek painted pottery has been discovered at foundation level in both these temples.

In the VI century the Etruscans—even if not in a bellicose way—were pushing southwards and threatening to expand their commercial

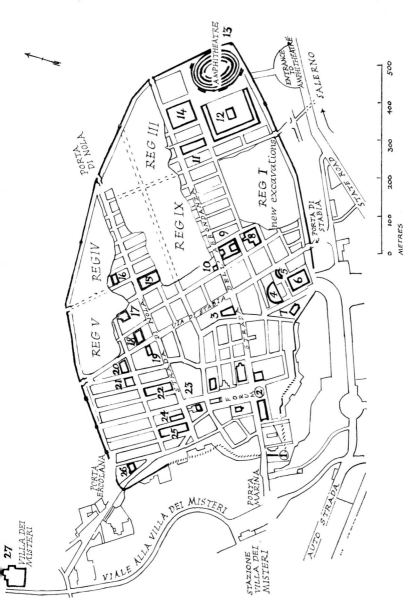

Fig. 11 Plan of Pompeii showing most important buildings.

5

centres at the expense of the Greeks. They had founded Capua and reached down towards the Sorrento peninsula. But by the end of the century the Romans and Latin peoples cut across their territory, isolating the southern from the northern Etruscans, whose influence in Pompeii diminished: in fact there is little or no sign of it.

The second period of Pompeii's history then began. The whole of Campania was gradually falling into the hands of the Samnites, a mountain people who spoke an Oscan dialect, and whose territory centred on the Benevento region. At the time of their approach Pompeii had recently been enlarged, and defensive walls built around it: it is to this phase that the more orderly street layout of all but the south-west corner belongs. The Pompeians, frightened at the thought of Samnite domination, pleaded to the Romans for protection, and were admitted into the Roman federation in the late IV century.

The town, whose history was not peaceful during the disturbed III century, grew slowly, and many of the relatively few houses were large with big gardens. By the II century the domination of the Romans was firmly established, and trade was opened up between the coastal towns of Campania and far-off countries, so that it is not surprising to find that the carefully planned layout of public buildings at Pompeii and elsewhere reflects the influence of Hellenistic cities. The Forum area was redesigned and embellished, public baths were built, and a temple set up to the Egyptian goddess Isis. Luxuries arrived from the East, slaves from Delos, and works of art, sometimes, perhaps looted from Greek towns by the Romans. Although the inhabitants of the town were still Italic, their houses at Pompeii were now predominantly of Roman type; no longer inward-looking and grouped round a loggia, in the native tradition, but with extra rooms opening off a garden court-yard or colonnaded peristyle. The richer people were able to afford their own bathrooms, though the water supply still came from wells. Less work was done inside the houses, for small shops and craftsmen had their premises nearby, so that weaving, baking, market-gardening, metal and leather working etc. were all practised in or near the town.

By the end of the II and early in the I century B.C. there was growing discontent against the Romans on the part of the inhabitants of native towns such as Pompeii. The walls were partially rebuilt, and defensive towers added, and even the able Sulla was unable to take it by siege. Signs of this siege remain to us in painted notices scrawled on some houses, directing the garrison to various parts of the defences. Eventually, obliged to slacken their rigid treatment, the Romans granted citizenship to the inhabitants of Pompeii and other cities, and also established a new colony there, so that in law, language, administration, in every way, it became Roman. As a sign of the new status, public buildings, a concert hall, public baths, an amphitheatre etc. were soon constructed, as well as a much-needed aqueduct.

The Pompeian market served all the surrounding countryside with fish, wines, cloth, etc. and a new prosperity developed. The houses grew more sumptuous with upper floors whose windows looked out on the busy streets; the decoration of mosaics and frescoes became increasingly rich, and it was many centuries before the standard of living was surpassed.

Pompeii and Herculaneum are unique in offering us the wonderful possibility of visualizing late republican and early imperial Roman towns obliterated in full life, for in the middle of all the bustle of daily activity, totally unprepared for its fate (Pompeii and Herculaneum had only recently recovered from an earthquake in A.D. 62), Pompeii was suddenly buried under a rain of ash and pumice stone on August 24th, A.D. 79, and although most of its inhabitants escaped, many others were overcome by fumes or trapped under the scorching material showered upon them. For us it is a moving experience to visualize the town before the disaster, and to read the notices chalked or painted on the walls when people were still untroubled. At the amphitheatre the spectators were assured that 'scent will be sprayed and awnings provided'; on the houses the inevitable Italian political slogans urge people to vote for C. Julius Polybius who 'stands for good quality bread', or for Marcellus 'who is backed by the farmers'. Today it is a town made even more dead by the fact that those of us who visit it are in it but not of it. It swarms with modern life and it is no longer possible for us to share the silence that Shelley felt when he wrote:

> 'I stood within the city disinterred;
> And heard the autumnal leaves like light footfalls
> Of spirits passing through the streets . . .'

Pompeii and Herculaneum live on in what they have handed down to the future, for the impact made by the discoveries in the 18th and early 19th century excavations so profoundly influenced the world of taste, that when one looks into Adam's library at Kenwood, or so many other interiors in Europe of that date, stucco-work, wall-paintings, even furniture might be replicas of Roman originals.

Practical information. Distance by autostrada from Naples 24 km. This is the best and quickest way of reaching Pompeii. Buses leave the Piazza del Municipio in Naples twice a day, and organized trips by pullman are arranged daily. There are also two railway stations at Pompeii: one, the *Villa dei Misteri* (service every half hour from the *Circumvesuviana*), and *Pompeii Scavi* (from the Ferrovia Naples-Salerno). Both take about half an hour.

Entrances. Most people go in by the Porta Marina, but there are other entrances at the *Amphitheatre, Porta Ercolano* and *Porta di Nola.*

Opening hours. From 9 till an hour before dusk. After 3 o'clock you pay a supplementary charge. During the summer (from June 1st to September 30th) the excavated area is again open from 8 to 11 p.m. and is partially illuminated. Custodians will unlock the various houses on request, but no photographs can be taken inside the houses without a permit. Authorized guides speak the principal languages, but it is advisable to buy a good guide-book which selects the more interesting houses to visit. The following notes have been designed to help those who do not want to spend more than a few hours in Pompeii.

There is a refreshment room etc. near the Temple of Jupiter (number 2 on the plan). All numbers refer to the plan (Fig. 11).

(1) THE ANTIQUARIUM

Room I. Pre-Samnite Pompeii (from IX–V B.C.). Architectural elements from the early temples etc. *Room II, Samnite Pompeii* (from 425–90 B.C.) During this period tufa from Nocera was predominantly used for sculptured details. Note especially the elements from a late III century B.C. temple dedicated to the Dionysiac deities, found outside the town, with an altar inscribed in Oscan. Between *Rooms II and III* is the statue of the Empress Livia, as well as a fine portrait of Augustus's adopted son Marcellus etc. *Rooms III and IV. Roman Pompeii.* Many small Roman objects and casts of burnt bodies.

Material illustrating crafts and technological apparatus in daily use. Models of the fine villa (now covered) at Boscoreale. (Note that most of of the fine mosaics, bronzes etc. from Pompeii are in the *Muses Nazionale* in Naples.)

(2) THE FORUM COMPLEX (see Fig. 12)

This was the centre of the town's civil and religious life and as time

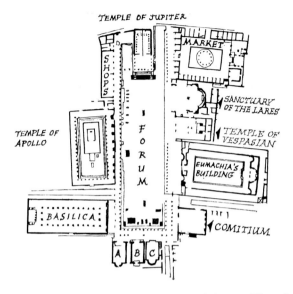

Fig. 12 Pompeii. Plan of the Forum Area (No. 2 on Fig. 11).

Plate 5 Pompeii. The Forum.

went on various public offices and other buildings grew up around it. It was originally surrounded on all sides but the north (where stood the Temple of Jupiter) by a portico, and part on the east side still retains its upper colonnaded loggia. Part of the Samnite-period trabeation remains on the south side, but most of the buildings were in course of reconstruction at the time of the final disaster. The Forum was ornamented in the customary way with statues and busts of distinguished persons.

The Basilica, a long rectangular building with a big colonnaded central hall, is the most imposing of all the public buildings in Pompeii, and was the centre of the town's economic activities, and also the place where commercial and civil law cases were brought to trial. It belongs to the pre-Roman period, about 120 B.C.

Three rooms (A, B and C) are at the south end and were used as municipal offices.

The Temple of Apollo. The site on which this stands had already been consecrated by the VI century B.C. but the portico belongs to the Samnite period, and the whole has been much re-handled. The bronze statues are copies of the originals now in the *Museo Nazionale* in Naples. The altar in front of the steps leading to the cella bears a Republican Roman inscription. There were shops and public lavatories in the vicinity.

The Temple of Jupiter is of Italic, not Roman, type with a wide cella and large pronaos surrounded by Corinthian columns. Built in about the mid-II century B.C., in Roman times it became the *Capitolium* dedicated to Jupiter, Juno and Minerva, but was badly damaged by the earthquake of A.D. 62; and was being restored at the time of the eruption.

The Macellum, or covered market, is of imperial Roman date. Around the inside were the various shops and premises used by the money-changers and shopkeepers. On the wall on the east side there are fragments of fine painted decoration. In many ways this building resembles the market known as the 'Temple of Serapis' at Pozzuoli.

Next to the *Macellum* is the *Sanctuary to the Lares*, and then comes the *Temple of Vespasian*, dedicated to the cult of the Emperor. It has a fine marble altar in the middle, decorated with scenes of sacrifice.

Edificio di Eumachia (Eumachia's building) is a large and impressive structure which, according to an inscription, was put up at the expense of a priestess Eumachia, as the headquarters of the corporation of dyers and cloth-makers. It was dedicated to Concordia Augusta, the personification of Augustus's wife Livia whose statue stood in the central apse at the far end inside. Beautifully decorated doorway.

The Comitium was used for the election of the city magistrates.

(3) *The Terme Stabiane* (public baths) are the earliest and best preserved in Pompeii. They date from the II century B.C. but have been modified at various times, and were in process of restoration when they were destroyed. The central courtyard, used for games, had the men's and women's public baths on the east side, and private baths behind the portico on the south. The west side was dedicated to the combined use of baths and exercises, and with rooms for undressing and for massaging with sand and oil.

(4) *The Teatro Grande.* This was an open-air building cut into the rock in about 200–150 B.C. and enlarged and altered in the Augustan period. The scene-building is characteristic of Roman theatres.

(5) *The Teatro Piccolo* (or Odeion), to the east of the bigger theatre, was a little covered building probably used largely for miming shows or concerts, and it was built just after 80 B.C. by two deserving magistrates who also paid for the Amphitheatre.

Behind the scene-structure of the *Teatro Grande* was a very spacious porticoed square (6) originally designed for the spectators in the intervals, but which was later modified for the use of gladiators. It was surrounded by many small rooms on two floors.

(7) *Triangular Forum with a Doric temple and public fountain.* The temple, originally dedicated to Heracles, was put up in the VI century B.C. when Pompeii was strongly influenced by Greeks from Cumae and Neapolis (Naples). There are remains of its terracotta revetments in the Antiquarium (see number 1 on the plan). Under the Romans its dedication was changed to Minerva. This temple, much altered and destroyed, is only interesting for its historic significance.

(**8**) *The Casa del Menandro* (or *del Tesoro*) was called after a portrait of the Greek poet Menander found there, or, as its alternative name implies, after the big collection of silver table-ware discovered in one of its cellars, and now displayed in the *Museo Archeologico* in Naples. This splendid house is richly decorated, and its atrium is painted in the Fourth style (described on p. 58). Apart from the large rooms for the use of the family, there were also domestic quarters. On the east side are bathrooms with delightful mosaics.

(**9**) *The Casa del Criptoportico*. This has a little stairway leading down to a covered gallery or cryptoporticus under the garden. At the time of its destruction this house was in process of being adapted as a wine cellar but this was never completed. The vaulted roof is stuccoed and there are frescoes in the Second style (see p. 58). Scenes from the *Iliad* and other poems decorate the frieze. There is a rather macabre collection of gesso casts of the bodies of the occupants who were overcome by fumes. The *salone tricliniare* was also decorated in the Second style with some lovely still-lifes.

(**10**) *The Officina di Verecundus* was a factory for felt and woollen stuffs, under the divine protection of Mercury and Pompeian Venus, a painting of whom, in 4-horsed chariots, is near the entrance. There are some fascinating painted scenes of the work taking place in the factory, the selling of the cloth etc.

(**11**) *The Casa di Loreius Tiburtinus*. This is a richly decorated house with a magnificent garden which probably belonged to a patrician family from Rome. There is a long loggia with a portico and with a small temple in the centre of a court with ornamental marble statuettes. Opening off this loggia are the main rooms, one with a fine frieze painted with scenes from the *Iliad* etc. On the east side of the house is a room with decorations on a white ground, characteristic of the Fourth style (see p. 58). The garden is specially pleasing, with a charming fountain. At one side of the garden the imprints of large fruit trees were found.

(**12**) *The Palaestra* (Palestra Grande) is of imperial Roman date. It functioned as a gymnasium and was evidently built to take the place of the Palestra Sannitica (Samnite Palaestra) which had become too small. (This stood behind the auditorium.)

(**13**) *The Amphitheatre* is important largely for its early date, about 80 B.C. There is a vivid Roman painting of this building in the *Museo Nazionale* in Naples showing the scenes of violence which are known to have broken out there in A.D. 59 between people from Nocera and Pompeii, and which were so serious that the games were prohibited for ten years. Capable of holding 12,000 spectators, it is a simple structure lacking the complicated underground passages and hauling devices as at Pozzuoli and at Santa Maria di Capua Vetere (see p. 78 and p. 80). Two inscriptions under the decorative niches by the north entrance seem to refer to restorations after the earthquake of A.D. 62. Seats for important personalities were reserved in the first and second order of seats, and according to a decree by Augustus, the upper gallery was for women. The big stone rings at the very top of the cavea were for holding the awning, shown in the painting.

(**14**) *Villa di Giulia Felice.* This is a large and unusual villa made up of three parts: the living-quarters, a bath building which had been turned over to public use, and a set of rooms let off for eating-places and small shops entered from Via dell' Abbondanza or from the little street on the west. A *triclinium* with marbles from decorated beds is below the west side of the portico. A fine still-life came from the house and is now in the *Museo Nazionale* in Naples. This house is characteristic of the many which had to be divided up to accommodate people left homeless by the earthquake.

(**15**) *Casa del Centenario,* so called because it was excavated 1800 years after the eruption destroyed it. It is a very complex building uniting three originally independent houses. It has a very large garden once ornamented with a statue of a satyr with a wineskin (*Museo Nazionale,* Naples). Good paintings and mosaics in many of the rooms.

(**16**) *Casa di Marco Lucrezio Frontone.* It belonged to the early years of the Empire, partly restored. There are pleasant decorations, some belonging to the Third style (see p. 58) and in perfect condition and mostly of mythical scenes, in many of the rooms. In the garden the first room on the right has a painting of Pyramus and Thisbe, and Bacchus and a Silenus.

(**17**) *Casa delle Nozze d'Argento* is one of the finest patrician houses, originally of the Samnite period but altered in Roman times. Atrium decorated in the Second style (see p. 58). Most of the best rooms are round the south side of the peristyle.

(**18**) *Casa del banchiere Lucio Cecilio Giocondo*, famous for the discovery of a number of receipts on wax tablets. Inside to the left of the atrium some interesting marble reliefs show the Temple of Jupiter and the Triumphal arch which stood nearby, and other buildings destroyed in the A.D. 62 earthquake. Some fine painted decoration in the Third style (see p. 58).

(**19**) *Casa di Vesonio Primo* originally of the Samnite period but rebuilt in the Augustan period. The walls at the end of the peristyle are painted with a big picture of Orpheus.

(**20**) *Casa degli Amorini Dorati*. This belongs to the period of Nero and is one of the best-preserved houses, which may have been lived in by Nero's wife's family. Theatrical masks are the dominating motif of the decorations. There is a beautiful peristyle with its west end raised like a stage, and with marble masks between the columns. The occupant evidently loved artistic things and had leanings towards oriental religion, as there is a shrine to Isis in one corner of the portico. In the north portico there is a big room with remains of its ceiling, leading into a room decorated with Cupids engraved in gold foil covered with glass discs.

(**21**) *Casa dei Vettii* is one of the most luxurious houses of the latest phases of Pompeii and belonged to enriched merchants. Nearly all the fine wall decorations are in the Fourth style (see p. 58). The *triclinium* is sumptuously decorated in Pompeian red with mythological scenes. In order to protect the paintings the roof has been restored. The garden with its marble ornamentation and fountains has been studied in detail, for the flowers which were growing there have left the imprints of their roots, and so the exact position of the flower-beds is known.

(**22**) *Casa del Fauno*. (See Fig. 13.) This takes its name from the statue of the little dancing faun now in the *Museo Nazionale* in Naples (Room IX). One of the finest houses we know from the Roman world, this house may have been lived in by Sulla's nephew. It was originally built in the Samnite period (II century B.C.) when Hellenistic influence was

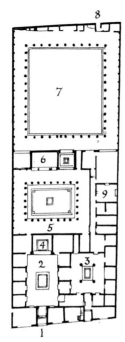

Fig. 13 Pompeii. Plan of the Casa del Fauno.

strong, and it therefore reflects a fusion of Italic and Hellenistic taste. Above the entrance (1) is written a welcoming greeting. Small bedrooms are grouped around the first atrium (2) which now has a reproduction of the original statue of the faun. To the north of the atrium is a small room (4), perhaps a *tablinum* where archives were kept, and on each side of it were rooms thought to be *triclinia* or dining-rooms. Another rather smaller atrium (3) lies off to the right. Continuing through the house you reach a fine peristyle (5) with a kitchen (9) on its east side. This peristyle leads on to a much larger one (7) with two superimposed orders of columns on its south side. The room marked (6) on the plan was originally very splendid and its floor was covered by the magnificent mosaic of the battle between Alexander the Great and Darius (see *Museo Nazionale*, Room LXI). It had stuccoed columns painted to represent porphyry. A small back entrance is at the north end of the house (8).

(**23**) *The Terme del Foro* (Forum Baths), entered from the Via delle Terme, date from about A.D. 80. Divided in the usual Roman manner into separate sectors for men and women with a single heating system for the whole, the complex has a wonderfully preserved *caldarium* in the men's sector, and a *tepidarium* which has a stuccoed vaulted roof and terracotta telamones in niches. The most striking effect is given by the big brazier, and the bronze seats inscribed with the donor's name, and a large marble basin with an inscription in bronze lettering giving the names of the two magistrates who paid for it: it belongs to the first few years A.D. These baths are also equipped with a palaestra surrounded by a portico.

(**24**) *Casa del Poeta Tragico* (made famous from Bulwer-Lytton's *Last Days of Pompeii*) belongs to the latest phase of the town's life, and is decorated with marvellous frescoes, and some good mosaics. There are paintings of mythological scenes, but the best of them (Zeus and Hera on Mount Ida) and several others are now in the *Museo Nazionale* in Naples.

(**25**) *Casa di Pansa* is a very large house occupying the whole of an *insula* and was originally built in the Samnite period. The last owner, however, like so many owners of big houses in Pompeii after the earthquake, had subdivided it into various flats and shops for letting. Its big garden is now used for growing plants.

(**26**) *Casa del Chirurgo.* An important house for two reasons; first because it is one of the best examples of an early Pompeian house (Samnite period, IV–III century B.C.) and secondly because it produced the most complete evidence for Roman surgical, or maybe more correctly veterinary, instruments (now on show in the *Museo Archeologico* in Naples, *Room XCV*). Apart from the houses and public buildings described above, there are innumerable shops, craftsmen's premises and prostitutes' quarters.

(**27**) *The Villa dei Misteri* is outside the walls, and is entered separately up a drive with a limited parking space. It is a very large and important villa, chiefly famed for its truly outstanding mural paintings which will be briefly described here. For the rest of the building it need only be said that it was originally built in the I century B.C. and that from a relatively unimportant dwelling it was enlarged into a patrician house

After the earthquake, however, it was partly adapted for more modest inhabitants, probably to provide accommodation for the many homeless people.

The important room is called the *Sala del Grande Dipinto*, reached to the right of a smaller room just after you enter. The great paintings on all the walls form one complete unit, and are thought to have been painted by a Campanian painter of the late I century B.C. or early Ist century A.D., added to a background painted in the Second style (see p. 58). Although the theme of the painting is still under discussion, it is thought to represent the initiation of a bride into the Dionysiac mysteries. Starting with the wall on the left as you enter, the scenes are thought to represent the following: (1) a child reads the sacred rites in the presence of two adult women. (2) a priestess and two servants making a sacrifice. (3) Silenus playing a lyre in a pastoral scene. (4) a woman about to be initiated is terrified by a winged demon who is scourging a young woman. (5) group of two satyrs and a Silenus with a mask. (6) the sacred marriage of Dionysus and Ariadne, symbolic of the bliss awaiting the initiated. (7) the unveiling of the sacred basket containing a covered phallus. A winged figure making a forbidding gesture with a *flagellum*. (8) the flagellation of the young woman in expiation. The young woman seeks refuge in the lap of a companion. (9) orgiastic dance of the young Bacchante. (10) the dressing of the bride for the initiation ceremony. (11) a seated woman who has already been initiated.

In an important paper given to the British Academy, Professor Zuntz challenges the accepted interpretation, and denies that the rites of the initiation are depicted at all in this painting, or that the girl is uncovering the phallus, and suggests that she is rather protecting it as a result of seeing the threatening demon. His reasoning is too long to enter into here. But he concludes, after careful analysis of the meaning of each figure, that the painting is a copy with various alterations of a Greek original which may have been in the Sanctuary of Dionysus at Pergamon. But the present painting selects and alters what it requires from the original, and this suggests that the Roman occupants of the villa added certain figures and adapted the painting to fit their concept which differed from the Greek one. The girl about to be flagellated wears no ring, and extra-marital relations may incur divine punishment. It is interesting in this context to note that the Emperor Augustus made every effort to restore the sanctity of marriage.

Pozzuoli

This town, called *Puteoli* by the Romans, was originally a Greek town which, together with Cumae, stood as an outpost of Greek culture on the southern edge of the Etruscan area of penetration and influence. During the late republican and early imperial periods its harbour played an extremely active rôle, especially for the reception of commercial goods destined for Rome and other cities coming from the Near East and Alexandria, and it is therefore no surprise to learn that St. Paul landed here from an Alexandrian ship. One must picture the town bustling with sailors and cosmopolitan life, often the scene of the official reception or departure of emperors or distinguished men of state on their way to or from Rome. From Puteoli they followed a short road which linked the town with the Via Appia. In the course of time the town grew very wealthy and Cicero had a villa here and referred to it as 'little Rome'. Hadrian died here and not long after, when Trajan had rebuilt the port of Ostia to serve Rome more conveniently, Puteoli gradually lost its importance. A Christian colony was already existing there when St. Paul disembarked in A.D. 61.

There is an *Antiquarium* in Via del Serapeo, open from 9 to 4. It contains sculptures, inscriptions etc. from Pozzuoli, Cumae and Baiae. Two other buildings are unusually interesting: the so-called 'Temple of Serapis' and the Amphitheatre.

The *'Temple of Serapis'* is near the Antiquarium, and can be visited from 9 to 4. It is not really a temple but a Roman public market (*macellum*), of a type well known throughout the Roman world. Built in the Flavian period with later additions, it has suffered much from the fluctuations of the water level. It was laid out as an open courtyard in the centre of which stood a fountain covered by a cupola supported on Corinthian columns of African marble. This open area was bordered on all sides by shops, opening alternately either into the internal portico, or into the surrounding streets. Across the court from the entrance a large projecting apse contained the statue of Serapis, while decorative niches probably held statues of the divine protectresses of the town's prosperity and trade. On the same side, in the corners of the market, old drawings showed exceptionally well-preserved public lavatories.

The Amphitheatre, entered from a turning off Via Solfatara, was one of the most magnificent and interesting in all Italy. Built by Vespasian in the 1st century A.D. to replace a smaller one of Augustan date nearby, it was capable of holding some 40,000 spectators.

The four main entrances were originally surmounted by monumental inscriptions recording how the great amphitheatre was built at the public expense of the city. Now shorn of many of its distinguished elements, it is still especially important today for its unusually well-preserved and complex substructures which were probably added at about the time of Trajan or Hadrian.

From the present entrance on the east side you can descend into the underground area by the two steep ramps down which must have been hauled not only much of the apparatus needed for the shows, but also the cages containing the wild animals which were to be exhibited. Once these were safely inside, the ramps were closed by massive oak doors. The subterranean area is divided into rooms and corridors, the middle one of which led to a large opening in the centre of the arena. This was used for the setting up of scenery etc. and was covered during performances. Around the edge of the arena a series of rectangular apertures served to give light to the underground corridor skirting the edge of the arena; these apertures, too, were closed during performances. Alongside this corridor is a whole series of small dark rooms arranged on two superimposed levels under the podium of the auditorium; the upper rooms served for the wild animals who were let out of their cages into the arena which was landscaped to form sandy hills with groups of palm trees to provide a naturalistic setting for the displays.

Santa Maria Capua Vetere (Roman *Volturnum*)

This town, standing on the northern limits of the area treated in this book (Capua comes within the volume on Central Italy), was founded by the Etruscans in around 600 B.C. and was sacked by the Samnites in 423 B.C. Volturnum later became the capital of Roman Campania, described by Livy as *urbs maxima opulentissimaque Italiae*. Hannibal spent the winter here in 216–215 B.C. after the townspeople had opened their gates to him after his victory at Cannae, but subsequently Volturnum again fell into Roman hands and was much reduced both in size and importance. It did not regain full prosperity until the time of the emperors, but it then boasted a walled perimeter of 6 miles, with 7 gateways, 2 forums, 2 theatres, a *circus*, public baths, numerous temples and the huge amphitheatre with its associated school for gladiators.

The town still retains its early grid street plan, a Flavian arch, one of the largest amphitheatres in all Italy, and a specially well-preserved Mithraeum. The Duomo incorporates many ancient sculptural details. There are two unusually interesting Roman tombs just outside the town on the road to Caserta (see below).

The Flavian Arch (Arco di Adriano) stands at the end of Corso Umberto I, once on the Via Appia. It appears to have been built in honour of Hadrian who had carried out basic alterations and additions to the amphitheatre. Only one much despoiled outer arch still remains of what was once a triple arch faced with marble.

The Amphitheatre (Piazza I Ottobre). (Plate 6.) Opening hours vary according to the season, and it is often closed as early as 3 o'clock. The same ticket allows you to visit the Mithraeum in a street about ten to fifteen minutes away on foot.

The date of the original building is not accurately known, but it must have been constructed by the colony sent to the town at the time of Augustus. Part of an inscription in the museum at Capua refers to its restoration by Hadrian and its embellishment by Antoninus Pius. In later centuries it has been despoiled for building stone, but it has many features which make it one of the most interesting of Italian amphitheatres. It is a very large structure of elliptical plan, entered from the south, and originally it stood four stories high on the outside. Each of the lower three stories had 80 arches, some ornamented with busts or statues of various divinities. (A number of these are built into the façade of the Palazzo Municipale in Capua.) The upper storey was so contrived that it was able to carry an awning or *velarium* to protect the spectators from the sun or rain. These awnings may have been a Campanian invention of as early as 70 B.C. and according to Lucretius they were sometimes gaily painted. One is shown in a painting from Pompeii. Apparently the *velarium* was sometimes manipulated by sailors standing on the roof of the colonnade above the upper tier of seats.

The subterranean passages below the arena, sometimes showing signs of painting, are very similar in design to those of Pozzuoli (see p. 79) and were provided with many corridors and storage places as well as elevators for the scene decorations and the animals' cages.

Plate 6 S. Maria Capua Vetere. Amphitheatre showing underground
structures.

It was in this area that Spartacus massed the rebellious slaves in the
great revolt of 73 B.C.

The Mithraeum (off Via Morelli) see Plate 7, must be unlocked for you by
the custodian from the amphitheatre, is about 10–15 minutes away on
foot if you have no car. It is a quite exceptionally well-preserved example
and very well worth seeing. It is an underground vaulted chamber built
in the 2nd or 3rd century A.D. with a painted roof, and on the end wall a
large painting of Mithras killing the bull. Along the walls are benches
for the worshippers, and above these are all that remains of frescoes
thought to have shown the seven stages leading up to the state of
spiritual perfection to which the cult aspired. The worship of Mithras,

Plate 7 S. Maria Capua Vetere. Mithraeum interior with painting of Mithras killing the Bull.

which entailed a system of secret rites and mysteries, originated in Persia and became a serious rival to Christianity in the early centuries A.D. It was first introduced into Rome in 68 B.C. and gradually gained a wide following all over the Empire. There are notable examples in Rome, Ostia, Osterbrücken in Germany and elsewhere including England. The main theme of the religion which, unlike Christianity, was founded on a mythical founder, first mentioned in the Veda, was the constant struggle between good and evil.

Just outside the town on the road to Caserta, one on each side of the road, are two interesting and well-preserved Roman tombs. One is a conical and rather baroque building of the 2nd century, known as the *Conocchia*, and the other, slightly nearer Santa Maria Capua Vetere, is the largest Roman tomb in Campania. (See Plates 8A and B.)

Those interested in the early Christian period may like to visit the small chapel at San Prisco 2 km. away: it is in the Chiesa Madre or Duomo, and has some unusually fine mosaics of the 6th century. The altar is a re-used Roman marble bath.

Plate 8A Roman tomb outside Santa Maria Capua Vetere.

Plate 8B Roman tomb of La Cannocchia outside Santa Maria Capua Vetere.

Not far away again is the impressive Romanesque church of Sant'
Angelo in Formis, built on the ruins of a Campanian temple dedicated
to Diana.

Sorrento (ancient *Surrentum*)

This was an early Italic settlement which may have been occupied
for a time as a trading post by the Etruscans, and subsequently by both
the Samnites and Romans. Like Baiae and Ischia and so many places
around this coast, it became a holiday resort and retiring place for rich
Romans in late republican and early imperial times.

In the *Museo Correale di Terranova*, in Via Correale leading off
Piazza Tasso, there are some important medieval objects, but the few
prehistoric, Roman and Greek finds are of minor significance.

Vesuvius

There are excursions to Vesuvius which is reached by road from
Resina near Herculaneum, and then the last stretch up to the crater
is made with a guide. The crater is about 200 metres deep.

In early Roman times it was regarded as extinct and Strabo actually
wrote that it was so only sixty years before the eruptions which
destroyed Pompeii and Herculaneum and damaged Stabiae.

2 · THE TAVOLIERE, THE GARGANO PENINSULA AND THE VULTURE

Arpi, Ascoli Satriano, Avellino, Barletta, Benevento, Canne della Battaglia (Cannae), Canosa di Puglia, Foggia, Larino, Lucera, Manfredonia, Melfi, Mirabella Eclano, Ordona, Salpi, Siponto, Venosa.

The country changes very abruptly after crossing the Apennines from Benevento into northern Apulia, for here one enters the so-called Foggia plain or *Tavoliere*, a flat, rather uninteresting land which takes its name from a chessboard, a name suggested by its appearance because the Romans had divided it up with large square areas under their agricultural system of centuriation. This plain is bordered on the south by the Ófanto river (the Roman *Aufidus*), the crossing of which was frequently disputed in ancient times, particularly at the battle of Cannae when Hannibal inflicted his great defeat on the Romans. To the east of Foggia lies the high land of Monte Gargano, a wooded limestone promontory, as yet but little explored archaeologically, so it need not be described here. In recent years an important Upper Palaeolithic cave has been discovered there, the Grotta Paglicci, near Rignano Garganico, with polychrome paintings of horses and hands, and the peninsula has also produced Beaker sherds.

In contrast with the Gargano peninsula, the Tavoliere offers enormous archaeological promise, for air photographs have shown that in prehistoric times it was densely populated: its relatively unwooded character and its marshes abounding in fish and wild fowl must have attracted these early settlers, some of whom may well have come from the other side of the Adriatic, which with a following wind can be reached without a very arduous journey. So far, the most important of these prehistoric sites is that of Coppa Nevigata not far from Manfredonia, near the great salt marsh of Lake Salpis which has now been largely drained. This same area was also of considerable prominence in Daunian times when Greek settlers, too, reached the area, and Salpi, with the possible exception of Spina, a little to the north of Ravenna, is the most northerly of their colonies on this coast. The Daunians were one of the so-called Iapygian tribes settled in Apulia, and their land marched with that of the Peucetians perhaps at the Ófanto river. Only

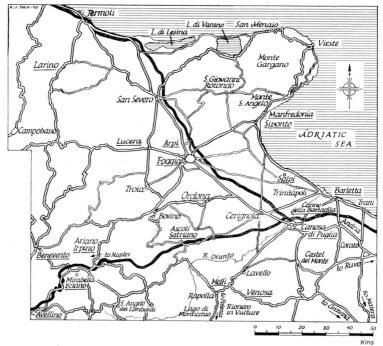

Fig. 14 Map of the Tavoliere, the Gargano Peninsula and the Vulture.

recently excavations have begun to reveal something of the character and culture of these people. (See Manfredonia.)

The third area in this map lies to the south and comprises the volcanic heights of the Monte Vulture with its characteristic lakes and huge extinct craters. This once barren and wild country, now cultivated and delightful, once marked the boundaries of the Samnites to the west, the Daunians to the east, and the Lucanians to the south.

Venosa has given its name to a Clactonian phase of the Palaeolithic, richly represented there.

For centuries the Tavoliere had an almost steppe-like and marshy appearance with, after prehistoric times, a relatively sparse population; today it is flourishing under arable and vineyards, and many of the malaria-infested marshes have been drained. These marshes once delighted the Emperor Frederic II as a hunting ground, and owing to his need for hunting lodges or castles and to his desire to embellish his beloved Apulia he instigated the building of many castles and churches

—importing Arab craftsmen from Sicily where he had been brought up, and oriental architectural conceits from the Middle East which he had visited in the Crusades. There are notable castles of various dates throughout the area treated in this chapter: at Castel del Monte (the most sophisticated of Frederic II's castles), at Lucera and Barletta; and particularly interesting churches and cathedrals at Benevento and Troia, and at Trani, Barletta and Santa Maria di Siponto on the coast etc. One of the most remarkable buildings to be found in the western world is that of Bohemond who fought in the Crusades and had his tomb made in Canosa di Puglia (see p. 102).

Archaeologically speaking, from the point of view of visible monuments the area covered in this chapter is perhaps disappointing. But it has admirable museums both at Foggia and at Benevento, and at the latter town two Roman monuments of great merit—the richest Roman arch to remain to us, and the Roman theatre. At Canne della Battaglia you can study the maps of the battle of Cannae and see objects from the hill-town nearby, and there are other not very spectacular Daunian and Roman sites. The famous decorated Daunian stelae are soon to be displayed in Manfredonia. The rich and complex IV century tombs at Canosa di Puglia, a famous centre for the very individual local pottery made there at the time, are also well worth visiting.

Arpi (near Arpi Nova—ancient *Arpino* or *Argirippa*)

A few kilometres to the north-east of Foggia lie the remains of the early town of Arpino, described, almost surely exaggeratedly, by Strabo as 'the largest, with Canusium, of the Italiot cities, as is clear from the circuit of the walls'. But, today, people hoping to see much of this once impressive Daunian town are disappointed to find little more than sparse remains of some Hellenistic houses. Excavations are, however, taking place and in the near future the site may well be worth visiting.

The town, whose harbour was at Siponto, was first mentioned during the Roman wars against the Samnites, when its inhabitants, fighting for the Romans, sent supplies and provisions for the siege of *Luceria* in 320 B.C. During Pyrrhus's campaign it remained faithful to Rome to whose cause it contributed a large contingent of cavalry and foot-soldiers. In 217 during the Second Punic War, Hannibal devastated all the surrounding countryside, yet in spite of this the gates were opened to him after his victory at Cannae, fought at no great distance away. Four years later the Romans re-took it as a result of treachery, but it was so repeatedly fought over during these wars that, impoverished, it never really picked up again. Its only mention is when Caesar halted for the night once when marching south to Brindisi.

Important finds from here, mostly from tombs, are in the museum at Foggia where photographs and plans explain the history of the town. (See p. 104.)

Ascoli Satriano (for archaeologists only)
(perhaps the ancient *Satricum* destroyed by the Samnites, and then refounded as the Roman *Ausculum*)

There is not a lot to see today in Ascoli Satriano, other than the remains of a Roman bridge over the Carapello (below the town coming from Foggia), and a Roman arch (ask for the Valle dell' Arco) and a very ruined aqueduct. But in the municipio there is a small archaeological collection dedicated mostly to finds from the indigenous necropolis of the IV–III century. There are other finds in the *Museo Civico* in Foggia. It was here that Pyrrhus won a victory over the Romans in 279 B.C.

Avellino (ancient *Abellinum*)

The site of the early town is not at Avellino itself, but about two miles to the east at Civita, outside Atripalda, where excavations have recently been made. For the archaeologist the **Museo Irpino** is the point of greatest interest. It is soon to be moved to Via Roma, near the Villa Comunale. Opening hours are irregular, but at the time of going to press they were as follows: Tuesdays, Thursdays and Saturdays 10–1.30; Mondays and Fridays 3–6.30; Sundays 9.30–12.30; closed on Wednesdays. This museum houses the Zigarelli collection with the addition of more recent finds from local excavations. Important objects come from the Copper Age necropolis of Mirabella Eclano near Taurasi—a group of tufa-cut oven-shaped tombs entered from a shaft, rather like the well-known tombs from Gaudo near Paestum. Other very important discoveries come from La Starza at Ariano Irpino. Iron Age grave-goods come from Cairano and various sites in the Ófanto valley, and some most interesting votive objects (VI to III century B.C.) are from the Sanctuary of the goddess Mephitis near Rocca San Felice: note especially some wooden figures. This sanctuary was mentioned by Cicero, Pliny and other early writers. It was on the site of a volcano in the last stages of extinction with gas emanating from a lake. There are many Samnite vases in the museum and a number of Roman funerary reliefs and a 1st century circular marble altar from Atripalda with scenes showing the Emperor Tiberius sacrificing to the deified Augustus and Germanicus.

The sanctuary of Montevergine can be visited from Mercogliano from which there is an elevator. This 12th century sanctuary was built in a magnificent position on the site of a temple of Cybele, and is now a major tourist attraction.

Barletta

The coastal town of Barletta, on the borders of ancient Daunia and Peucetia, probably had its origin in Roman times but it enjoyed its moment of greatest prosperity during the Middle Ages. It is worth visiting for its Burgundian Gothic Duomo, and other early churches including the Romanesque San Sepolcro, its Norman and later Castle, the so-called *Colossus* (the great bronze statue of imperial Roman times) and its Museum and Art Gallery near the junction of Via Garibaldi and Via Cavour.

The Colossus (Plate 9) standing outside, beside the church of San Sepolcro, is a huge bronze statue, nearly three times life size. Though it is sometimes popularly held to represent Hercules, it almost surely

Plate 9 Huge bronze statue of the Emperor Valentinian at Barletta.

portrays the Emperor Valentinian I who reigned from 364 to 375. Such enormous statues are not uncommonly found in the late Roman period, and this very fine example must have come from the Eastern Empire, shipped from Constantinople by Venetians in the 13th century and left in Barletta when their ship was wrecked off the coast there. The feet and hands are later replacements and the cross is also a subsequent addition.

The Castle was begun in Norman times and then twice enlarged, first in the 13th century, and then in the 16th by Charles V.

The Museum (Via Cavour) is probably to be transferred to the Castle and is open weekdays 9–1 and 5–7; Sundays 9–12. It contains much material from the Barletta area, particularly from Daunian sites of the V to III century. Finds from graves include large figured platters of the type made at Canosa, and vases of Gnathian type (see p. 122 and Plate 22B). From Canosa itself there is a big askos with the head of a Gorgon, and various red-figured vases. Important late V century krater probably painted by the Amykos painter. Other kraters of Apulian type show mythological or legendary figures. Note a fine ivory pyx decorated with a Bacchic procession: it is thought to have come from Pompeii.

In the *Danazione Cafiero* there are various objects collected from Etruria, small bronzes, gold ear-rings etc.

Benevento (Roman *Beneventum*)

Benevento stands on a hill which slopes down to the junction of two rivers; all around are mountains and radiating valleys. Being so well placed, it was chosen first as the chief town of the Hirpini (one of the sub-tribes of the Samnites) and then as a large town and focal point of communications by the Romans. The Via Appia had already reached it in republican times, and a couple of centuries later the Via Traiana was constructed under Trajan, whose triumphal arch marking the starting-point of the road's long journey to Brindisi and beyond is the main glory of Benevento today.

Little is known of its history before Roman times. Occasionally mentioned during the Samnite wars, its main claim to fame at about that time lay in its being the site of the final defeat of Pyrrhus fighting with the Samnites against the Romans in 275 B.C. In this battle, after which Pyrrhus returned to Greece, his elephants panicked and stampeded among his own men. During the Second Punic War, Hannibal had sacked it and it had changed hands several times between the Romans and the Carthaginians. In 268 B.C. Beneventum was made a Roman *colonia*, and during the Empire it attained a high degree of prosperity.

Today there are three places of achaeological interest to visit: Trajan's Arch, the Museum (*Museo del Sannio*) and the Roman theatre. There are also some good medieval buildings including the Duomo, the Castello, and the church and cloisters of Santa Sofia near the Museum.

Trajan's Arch (or the *Porta Aurea*) (Plates 10A and B) is one of the most impressive and richly decorated of the surviving Roman triumphal arches and was set up by the Roman Senate and people in honour of Trajan as *Optimus Princeps* on his departure to the Parthian War, and to commemorate the opening of the new version of the Via Appia, the so-called *Via Traiana*, in the year A.D. 114. Trajan never returned from his campaign and the arch was presumably finished by Hadrian whose political influence has been noted by scholars in some of the reliefs. As Sir Ian Richmond has written: 'It is the reliefs of the main façades that arrest attention and proclaim two distinct themes. The inhabitant of Beneventum or the traveller from Rome saw the glorification of Trajan's home policy for Rome and Italy: the traveller approaching from Brindisi and overseas was confronted by a façade proclaiming provincial policy and benefits.' The arch is made of limestone faced with Parian marble and is inscribed on both sides: IMP. CAESARI. DIVI. NERVAE. FILIO/NERVAE TRAIANO. OPTIMO. AUG./ GERMANICO. DACICO. PONT. MAX. ERIB./ POTEST. XVIII. IMP. VII. COS. VI. P.P. /FORTISSIMO. PRINCIPI. SENATUS. P.Q. R. Many of the reliefs are symbolic and their interpretation is open to discussion.

The external façade. The theme illustrated here is 'the settlement of the province, the making of treaties with the frontier folk, and the extension of Roman stock to people and defend the Empire'. The lower registers show on the left various Germanic tribal chieftains swearing loyalty to Trajan. The corresponding right hand panel may depict a Parthian embassy bringing gifts including a famous horse taught to kneel at command, and a mastiff led in by men with eastern haircrop introduced by Hercules, patron god of Parthia. As Richmond has pointed out, this emphasis on good relations with Parthia was Hadrian's rather than Trajan's policy. Above these panels are two others: that on the left shows Trajan receiving a recruit for the legions: that on the

Plate 10A Trajan's Arch at Benevento (detail).

Plate 10B Trajan's Arch at Benevento.

right depicts Trajan and *Mars Pater* presenting two small children to
Roma the city goddess (here shown with a plough symbolizing the
founding of new colonies). The children represent those who were to
be reared in the new colonies and the goddess *Abundantia*, shown with
the horn of plenty, refers to the good conditions under which they
would flourish. (According to another interpretation this scene shows
soldiers' children or orphans for whom Trajan had completed an
institution begun by Nerva. Under Trajan special loans were granted to
farmers and it is suggested that this explains the crowned figure of
Italia with a plough.) Of the top registers, that part where Trajan stood
has been partly destroyed. Protective gods of the Illyrian and Danubian
regions symbolize the Emperor's wars and granting of peace there; he is
being welcomed and accepted. The right-hand scene represents the
submission either of Mesopotamia, with the rivers Euphrates (left) and
Tigris (right), or of Dacia, with the Danube and another river.

The internal façade. One of the attic registers shows Trajan with
Hadrian beside him being received by two consuls, while behind them
Rome greets the Emperor. The other shows the Capitoline triad in the
foreground and Jupiter offering his thunderbolt to Trajan; in the background stand various tutelary deities of Roma. This whole scene is not
fully understood but it may refer to the conferment on Trajan of the title
Optimus Princeps, the full title of which was *Jupiter Optimus Maximus*.
The middle scenes represent the various benefits conferred by Trajan
on the people—the conferment of lands on veteran soldiers in the various
new colonies he had developed. The complementary panel refers to the
improvement in trade brought about by the Emperor, particularly to be
remembered for his work in the creation of new harbours and docks at
Ostia etc. Lower panels show Trajan's triumphal reception, after his
Germanic campaign, by the Roman people outside a colonnaded
building thought to be the Curia Julia.

In the passage way (west side) Trajan is shown sacrificing to inau-
gurate his new road. The complementary scene shows Trajan dis-
tributing charity funds to needy families and to various communities
represented by city goddesses.

The frieze of the arch shows scenes of a triumphal procession with
Trajan in his four-horsed chariot among animals to be sacrificed and
long processions with booty, and captives either walking or carried in
ox-carts or chariots—but the general theme of the Arch reliefs is not so
much to stress the territorial conquests of Trajan as his imperial

qualities: as Richmond notes: 'the emphasis is upon *optimus*, not *maximus*.' Again this 'is the sole example now surviving of a triumphal Arch which carries a complete scheme of decoration in the grand manner and which is intended to proclaim the relationship between an Emperor and his people, as opposed to a victory in war, external or internal'.

The Roman theatre (Via Port' Arsa). (Plate 11.) Opening hours 9 till dusk. This is quite an impressive building belonging to imperial times, and was begun by Hadrian and enlarged by Caracalla around the year A.D. 210. It has not yet been subjected to a full study as a good many modern buildings encroach on its peripheral area, and in fact have caused the destruction of the middle tier of seats in the auditorium. Much of the building was carried out in brickwork, but the seats and some other elements were faced with marble.

Behind the stage and stage-buildings ran a long marble-colonnaded peristyle reached by three regularly spaced flights of steps which may have led up from the Forum or other important public building. At

Plate 11 Benevento. Roman theatre.

each end of the peristyle which may have been used as a promenade by the spectators, were marble-decorated rooms, perhaps refreshment rooms. Behind the auditorium the lower corridor remains intact. It shows a strange feature in its large, irregularly placed brick-built niches, hardly suitable for decorative or storage purposes, and perhaps connected with the acoustics. Part of the stage set is still standing, with decorative niches at each side.

Above the upper tier of seats the arcade may have been decorated with the stone masks which can be seen among other fragments outside the ticket office, and here, too, are marble columns probably of Egyptian origin which may lead one to think that the famous Temple of Isis built by Domitian stood not very far away. (See Rooms V–IX in the Museum.)

In many respects this theatre is comparable to that built by Pompey in Rome and to the one at Pompeii.

The Museo del Sannio (Fig. 15) is housed in various rooms grouped around the Cloisters of Santa Sofia, off Piazza Matteotti. The entrance is to the right of the church. Opening hours: daily, except Mondays, 9–1. (Nearly everything of archaeological interest is on the ground floor.)

Fig. 15 Benevento. Plan of the Museum.

Fig. 16 Samnite gladiator of I B.C. from
Benevento.

Fig. 17 A Samnite warrior (from a bronze
in the Louvre).

Room IV. Prehistoric material. *Rooms V–IX.* Egyptian and neo-Egyptian sculpture from the Temple of Isis, built in A.D. 88 in Beneventum by Domitian, who had its dedicatory inscription written in hieroglyphs on an obelisk, and ancient statues brought specially from Egypt. *Room X.* Roman copies of Greek sculpture. *Room XI.* South Italian Greek and native wares of the V to III century B.C. Some of the leading Greek vase-painters are represented here, and there is an exceptional collection of III century B.C. vases from tombs near the Samnite town of Telesia. Terracotta sculptures and antefixes from VI century to Hellenistic times. *Room XII.* Hellenistic to Roman sculptures. *Rooms XIII–XVI.* Roman sculpture. Around the cloisters are Roman inscriptions etc. from I century B.C. to 6th century A.D. *Rooms XIX–XXI* house a reserve collection which can be visited on request. In *Room XXII* is a good collection of coins, Greek, Roman and later. (The post-Roman collections are on the First Floor.)

   Note that a few other Roman remains, mostly milestones, can be seen in the *Sezione Storica del Museo del Sannio*, in the Rocca dei Rettori (Castello).

Canne della Battaglia (site of the battle of Cannae)

Just before his famous victory in 216 B.C. Hannibal had marched south
through Luceria to the Ófanto river (the ancient *Aufidus*) to seize the
Roman supply depot at Cannae where remains of the native town can still
be visited (see below). The Roman army which confronted him was com-
manded on alternate days by two different generals, a curiously dangerous custom which was bound to play into Hannibal's hands. In recent
years the discovery of a big cemetery, thought to represent that of the
battle-slain, led to much discussion as to the exact site of the engage-
ment, but the burials were later proved to be men, women and children
of the 10th century. Certainly the conflict took place close to the Ófanto
river, for the crossing of this was a key problem in many campaigns of
different dates; but the river has often changed its course, the classical
texts do not specify if the fighting took place on its left or right bank,
and it must be admitted that it is doubtful if the exact site can ever be
established.

After Hannibal's victory his cavalry leader, who had been refused
permission to press straight on to Rome itself, is said to have turned to
his commander and said: 'Hannibal, you know how to win a battle, but
not to exploit it,' probably the remark of an imprudent man, for however much weakened the Roman forces were, the taking of Rome would
have entailed a long and difficult siege and the Roman fleet still com-
manded the seas. At all events Roman civilization survived, and as Livy
proudly wrote: 'The defeat at Cannae left Rome without a force in the
field, without a commander, without a single soldier. Apulia and
Samnium in Hannibal's hands, and now nearly the whole of Italy over-
run. No other nation in the world could have suffered so tremendous a
series of disasters and not been overwhelmed.' But Hannibal was insufficiently backed up by Carthage, and in fact this battle did not change the
course of history.

The Cannae Museum is interesting for the objects it contains from
excavations in the area, including finds from prehistoric times onwards.
It is intended to dedicate it largely to the Punic Wars.

On the Monte di Canne (or *Cittadella*) (Plate 12) are remains of a
Roman and medieval town, on a site previously occupied in prehistoric
times, and in the Museum there is a reconstructed section cut near the
gate of the town defences. This section has 15 different levels representing
3 or 4 principal phases. The town gate is on the east side of the hill, not

Plate 12 Canne (Cannae). Air view showing Monte di Canne near the site of
the battle.

far from the Museum. The walls belong to various dates beginning with
one built with big squared ashlars: the medieval ones are less regular.
Following the Via Principale, and running westwards, are a number of
Roman inscriptions and a milestone from the Via Traiana, inscribed in
honour of the Emperor who 'had the road built from Beneventum to
Brundisium at his own expense'.

The buildings belong to various phases of the hill's occupation, and
include a Christian basilica. Turning northwards from this you reach a
tall Roman granite column set up in recent years to commemorate the
battle.

To the south of the Museum there is an excavated area at Fontanella,
with remains of an Apulian village of the VI to III century B.C. and
earlier date.

Canosa de Puglia (Greek *Canusion*; Roman *Canusium*)

The hill town of Canosa di Puglia was an important centre on the
borders of Daunia and Peucetia, and its harbour at the mouth of the

Ófanto (perhaps at Barletta or Cannae) was mentioned by Strabo. It was well known in antiquity for its polychrome and red-figured vases and big askoi decorated with heads of women, horses or centaurs. In Augustus's time the inhabitants were bilingual, which suggests that the town had a Greek origin. It stood strongly for Rome in the Hannibalian wars and grew rich, largely on the production of wool, so that by the III century B.C. it was a really wealthy centre, which continued to prosper throughout imperial times, partly owing to the new commercial opportunities presented to it when the Via Traiana came into use.

But it is not only for its most ancient past that one visits Canosa today: many people will want to see the *Museo Civico*, the impressive IV century B.C. tombs known as the *Ipogei Lagasta*, and the Roman arch and tombs, but even more perhaps will want to visit the Cathedral, and the Tomb of Bohemond (son of Robert Guiscard, hero of the First Crusade). The latter building is a fascinating mixture of Byzantine and Arab architectural styles.

The Museo Civico (Piazza Martiri della Libertà—open by request in office hours at the Municipio where it is housed, and on Sundays from 10 to 12). It contains mostly Hellenistic and Roman finds from the district, particularly the curious locally made red-figure ware, and some so-called Gnathian ware (see Egnazia, p. 122) with its characteristic black ground and coloured patterns; objects from the Tomba D'Urso, found near the Arco Romano, a rich tomb whose remaining finds are in the Taranto museum.

Ipogei Lagasta (Plate 13) (custodian on site). These three typical Canosan tombs are reached by the Via Gen. Cadorna, and the biggest consists of nine chambers reached by a sloping passage leading into an atrium with painted and stuccoed Ionic columns. The burial chambers, designed to represent houses for the dead, have ceilings in which the rock is cut to imitate wooden beams, and in one of the tombs an imitation door has been cut in the rock. These tombs, which probably originated in the IV century B.C. but which were re-used at various later dates, are said to have contained richly adorned skeletons laid on gilded bronze beds decorated with ivory statuettes. Marble tables held the funerary food set out in rich platters and cups. Most of these finds can now be seen in the museum in Naples. It is sad that some other most interesting tombs with monumental façades of several stories have been destroyed.

Plate 13 Rock cut tombs (Ipogei Lagasta) at Canosa di Puglia.

The Arco Romano, sometimes called Porta Romana, belongs to the 2nd century A.D. It is now somewhat ruined and may originally have been faced in marble. Whether it was a gateway in the Via Traiana, which passed nearby, is doubtful: it may have been a funerary monument in the form of an arch, or a triumphal arch.

The Roman Mausoleum of Augustan date and the so-called *Torre Casieri* (a 2nd century A.D. tomb) are two of the remaining tombs alongside the Via Traiana. Other Roman tombs are near where the roads to

Lavello and Canne della Battaglia fork off: the biggest is called the *Monumento Bagnoli* and has two stories of which the upper is only partly preserved. It belongs to the 2nd century A.D.

Some of the columns built into the little church of S. Maria della Scala at Trani, are thought to have come from Roman buildings in Canosa.

The *Tomb of Bohemond*, with its magnificent bronze doors by Roger of Melfi, is attached to the Cathedral from which it is reached by a door in the South transept. Both buildings are of outstanding architectural interest for they reveal the very strong Arab influence in the Apulian Romanesque in the 11th and 12th centuries.

The zone now known as San Leucio is reached by taking a turning off the Andria road just outside Canosa. Here rather muddled excavations have revealed what appear to be remains of a IV century B.C. temple, overlaid by ruins of a 6th-century church with mosaic pavements etc.

Foggia

Though greatly ruined in the last war, and before that by an earthquake in 1731, Foggia is well worth visiting for its Museum and for the Norman cathedral which, though rebuilt in different styles, still retains its huge crypt with its four great supporting columns with Roman capitals. In the medieval period, particularly at the time of Frederic II, Foggia was a place of no small importance.

The Museo Civico, Piazza V. Nigri 4. Opening hours 9–1 and 4.30–7. Closed on Mondays. (See Fig. 18.)

This is a new and very selective museum with a reserve collection which is open to students by special arrangement. The prehistoric finds range from the Neolithic through to the Daunian period (contemporary with the Greek colonization of Southern Italy and Sicily) and into post-Roman times. A map of the main Daunian sites can be studied, and the collections are arranged typologically and chronologically as follows:

Room A. The typology of Daunian sites. Apulian red-figure pottery, and Gnathian wares (IV–III century) etc. Daunian wares of the VI century onwards with many examples of the characteristic handles modelled to represent human hands, animal heads etc. and decorated with simple floral or geometric designs. Pottery of the Canosan type

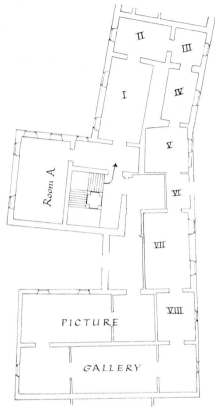

Fig. 18 Foggia. Plan of the Museum.

and of the Roman period. Coins, bronzes etc. This room is at present in course of arrangement.

Room I. During the Middle Neolithic period there was an intensive occupation of the flat plain around Foggia, and many of the villages have produced scratched and impressed pottery. One such village is Guadone di San Severo where, for the first time in Italy, the excavators have found big containers for conserving water. There is painted and impressed pottery from the ditch-enclosed villages of Passodi Corro, Amendola, San Vito etc. and air photographs show some of the great number of unexcavated villages of this period (over 200 of them) belonging to about the IV millennium B.C. The Late Bronze Age is represented by a site near the Madonna di Ripalta (Cerignola), where sub-Apennine ware was associated with pottery painted with geometric designs—a type which continued in use right up until the Roman colonization.

Four 'fossa' (trench) graves from Guadone di San Severo are especially interesting for their early date, for geometric and buccheroid wares were found together with VI century imported Ionian cups. From Arpi (see p. 87) are heads of stelae and bronze figurines, and there are photographs of other VII–VI century Daunian stelae, often anthropomorphic and showing many details of dress, daily life etc., which have recently been found in such numbers that they are now known to have been peculiar to Daunia. Bebore long, many will be on display in the Castello Manfredi museum at Manfredonia.

Rooms II and III are both dedicated to Arpi whose history and development are explained by finds and air photographs. *Room II* also contains finds from the 'Montarozzi' district rock-cut tombs (with entrance shafts) in which crouched burials were accompanied by locally made and Gnathian-type pottery dating from the VI to the III century. From the same district some 'fossa' graves, shown in *Room III*, yielded some indigenous pottery of the same date, and one or two imported vases and small objects, as well as two polychrome kraters, probably from a Canosan workshop. The corner cases exhibit various architectural elements from Arpi.

Room IV. Finds from Ordona (ancient *Herdoniae*), see p. 108. This was a Daunian town which flourished chiefly during the IV–III century B.C. Notice the bronze belts and decorated silver-plated diadem. A terra sigillata pot comes from a South Italian workshop. Other finds running through the Roman period and into the Middle Ages include many Arab coins.

Room V. San Paolo di Civitate (near ancient *Teanum Apulum*), Castelluccio di Sauri etc. Grave-goods from tombs at Teanum Apulum with VI–V century buccheroid wares etc. The contents of a grave from Castelluccio di Sauri include bronze spiral and other types of brooches.

Room VI. Siponto (ancient *Sipontum*) and Lucera (see pp. 109 and 105). Reconstructed stratified sequence of deposits found near the walls of Siponto. From Lucera there are statuettes and other votive offerings from a *stipe* at San Salvatore. Material from a private collection is in a corner case.

Room VIII. Ascoli Satriano (ancient *Ausculum*). (See p. 88.) Plans etc. of the excavated areas, and finds from the necropolis including some indigenous Daunian vessels with some rare imports.

Room VIII. Salpi (*Salapia*). In course of arrangement.

Rooms IX–XV contain the picture collection.

Larino (ancient *Larinum*)

The ancient site lies about 1 km. from the modern town, and was possibly the town of *Gereonium* where Hannibal camped before the battle of Cannae. The Roman town was at Piano San Leonardo where there are slight remains of an amphitheatre, some stretches of walls as well as some inscriptions and mosaics.

In the Municipio there is a small collection of archaeological objects, and some fine mosaic pavements, one showing the cave in which Romulus and Remus were said to have been suckled by the wolf.

Lucera (ancient *Luceria*)

There are several points of interest for the archaeologist in Lucera, a Roman amphitheatre and a museum as well as a medieval fortress and a 14th-century cathedral, some of whose smaller sculptural elements come from Roman monuments. Originally the town was a Daunian one, and it fell to the Samnites in the second war between that people and the Romans. It changed hands several times before 314 B.C., when it finally passed into Roman possession, and it enjoyed a particularly prosperous period in imperial Roman times. It is difficult to imagine the town as it was in the 12th–15th centuries, bristling with mosques and cupolas built by the thousands of Arabs installed there by Frederic II to work on his many castles.

The Roman amphitheatre. Coming from Foggia a main turning to the right into Viale Augusto leads you to the amphitheatre which according to an inscription was built in honour of Augustus and of the *colonia* of Lucera, on a site previously occupied by buildings of republican date overlying earlier tombs. It is an unspectacular and partly restored building characteristic of its period, with three central water-tanks in the arena.

The small Museo Civico Fiorelli, in Via De Nicastri 42, is opened on application to the custodian. Closed on Mondays. Note that the small Prehistoric Collection is in Room V.

Room I. Epigraphy. *Room II* a local collection of mostly Roman finds of the III–II century B.C. including ex-voto models of legs, feet, breasts etc., offered in request or thanks for cures.

Room III. Medieval. *Room IV* contains locally made portrait sculptures etc. *Room V.* Locally produced red-figure vases etc. and many small Roman objects. The prehistoric collection shown in this room includes Bronze Age pottery and stone implements from the Gargano. *Room VI.* Huge 1st-century mosaic pavement and a Roman copy of a Greek Venus.

Room VII. Coin collection, with interesting large clumsy Daunian coins.

See also the *Fortezza Angioina* built by 13th-century French and Italian masons, incorporating remains of Frederic II's Castle.

Manfredonia

Manfredonia is not an attractive place but you may see the new museum there, now being arranged in the Castello Manfredi, and it is also convenient for a visit to Siponto. At present there is a small museum in the *Biblioteca Comunale* near the Municipio, which houses finds from the prehistoric villages of Coppa Nevigata, Fontanarosa etc. which abound in the neighbourhood. At the time of writing, the Castello Manfredi is being arranged as a museum to contain, in particular, the remarkable series of VI–V century Daunian stelae or grave-slabs marking the position of cairns. These stones are carved to represent people, animals, ships etc. and are now being studied for the light they can throw on the dress and habits of the people who made them. They appear to be characteristic only of this northern part of Apulia, the ancient *Daunia*. Beneath the cairns the burials were laid in wooden coffins with their heads to the north on a paving of stones.

Melfi

The character of this little town of Melfi, even if it has changed somewhat from Edward Lear's time, is still one of great charm and character.
He described 'the picturesque buildings of the city (which seem to
occupy the site of some ancient place); the valley below it . . . the
numerous fountains; the innumerable caves in the rocks around . . .,
the crowded houses and the lofty spires of the interior: and the perfectly
Poussinesque castle with its fine corner tower commanding the whole
scene; so many fine features in a circumscribed space is not common to
see, even in Italy.'

Lear was right in thinking that Melfi had an early origin. It is
attested by the richly furnished tombs mostly of the V–IV century B.C.,
which were found to contain Greek geometric and red-figure wares, a
decorated bronze cuirass, a Corinthian helmet etc. There is a small
collection of prehistoric and later objects in the *Antiquario Civico* in the
Palazzo del Municipio and others are in the Castle. In the Palazzo del
Vescovado on the right of the Duomo, you can see the remarkably fine
marble sarcophagus, made in Asia Minor, probably dating from the
1st or 2nd century A.D., from the nearby village of Rapolla.

The Castle has been much re-handled but originated in Norman
times when the town enjoyed especial prosperity. This Castle was one
of Frederic II's favourite residences.

The Church of Santa Margherita is in a cave a short distance away,
near the cemetery, just off the road to Rapolla. It is worth visiting,
particularly for its 13th-century frescoes, and not far away is another
little rock-cut church called Santa Lucia.

The Cathedral, originally Norman, has been almost entirely rebuilt
but the lovely original Campanile still stands: it is decorated with
lava griffons, the emblems of the Norman dynasty.

Mirabella Eclano (ancient *Aeclanum*)

This was originally a Samnite city on the Via Appia. The ancient site
stands about 200 metres off to the right of the road as you approach
Mirabella from Avellino. Sacked by the Romans during the Social wars,

it was subsequently made a *colonia* under Hadrian, and it continued to be a place of some standing until the 7th century, after which a new town grew up on its ruins.

The Chiesa Matrice contains a rare 12th-century wooden crucifix, and a Roman inscription has been built into the base of the Campanile. There are slight remains of Roman public baths, houses etc. and a small *Antiquarium.*

Archaeologists may want to see the rock-cut tombs dating from about 1500 to 1100 B.C. of the Madonna delle Grazie, the finds from which are in the Antiquarium. To reach these tombs which have produced very rich finds, and which in some ways resemble the tombs at Gaudo near Paestum, take the road for Taurasi and after $3\frac{1}{2}$ km. you find the tombs on the right.

Ordona (for archaeologists only)
(ancient *Herdoniae*)

The remains of this early Daunian town of Ordona, which is thought to have been founded in the VI century B.C., stand on a little rise slightly to the north of modern Ordona, on the far side of the Bovino road. (Ask for the 'Scavi'.) Excavations have recently been made by the members of the Belgian Academy in Rome who have done much to ascertain the various phases of the town and its defences, and now archaeologists at least may like to visit it.

During its early history *Herdoniae* played an important part in the wars between Rome and Hannibal. Allied to Rome before war broke out, the town defected to Hannibal after his victory at Cannae, fought not far away. Twice the Romans tried unsuccessfully to recapture it, in 212 and 210, and its inhabitants were, in fact, always anti-Carthaginian in sympathy, so much so that Hannibal, disliking the attitude of some of its leaders, destroyed the town and transferred its inhabitants to Thurii and Metapontum. It was re-founded in the Roman republican period and entered its moment of major prosperity in the I century B.C.– 2nd century A.D. In 109 its position was enhanced as it stood on the cross-roads between the new Via Traiana and the Via Eclarense which led towards the territory of the Samnites.

The rather unimpressive remains to be seen today, for the most part on the east side of the hill, include a Roman period forum flanked by a colonnade, temples (one of which had an unusual square plan like the indigenous Italic ones) and a small amphitheatre, as well as some of the streets crossing at right angles and belonging to the Roman period layout beneath which was an earlier and more haphazard one. The Roman houses lining these streets were often provided with mosaic pavements and painted walls, whereas the underlying ones were smaller, and built with brick and river pebbles. Remains of an early church have also been uncovered, and an earthwork in the northern corner is now known to be post-Roman.

The town defences had seven successive phases, the earliest of them being made with sun-baked bricks in about 300 B.C. These were replaced by walls in *opus incertum* in the I century B.C. Almost their whole length can be made out and four gates, one at least flanked by towers. Near the forum were found some bases for statues of distinguished citizens of the town, with inscriptions recording their *cursus honorum.*

The finds from the necropolis throw much light on indigenous pre-Roman wares and are mostly in the museums of Foggia, Bari and Taranto.

Salpi (Greek *Salapia*)

The town of Salpi, which stood on the coast, gave its name to a big lake the *Salapina palus*, now mostly drained and an area of salt marshes. Very little is known of it except that it was apparently founded by Greeks including Rhodians, at an unknown date, and is perhaps the most northerly Greek colony on the east Italian coast. We know that in 214 B.C. Hannibal occupied it but it was retaken for the Romans four years later by Marcellus. In late republican times it was abandoned in favour of a new town on the western corner of the lake.

Excavations are taking place here but the remains of the Roman town are very slight. To reach this site take the road from Trinitàpoli towards Foggia for 6½ km. and then, where the Foggia road bends left and another leads on towards Zapponeta, take a lane leading north-east and ask for the Rovine di Salapia, or the Posta di Triglione, where there are slight traces of a large Hellenistic house and simpler buildings, as well as some big vats for olive pressing. Finds from Salpi are in the Foggia museum.

Siponto

Siponto is only 3 km. from Manfredonia. It is known to have once been an important Daunian town conquered by Hannibal and subsequently by the Romans. The site is marked by a granite column near some

ancient walling at Santa Maria di Siponto, Santa Maria being the
dedication of a Romanesque church of exceptional interest with a very
fine crypt. Nearby are the remains of an earlier basilica which may stand
on the site of a Temple of Diana, and a short way off is another
fascinating little Romanesque church dedicated to San Leonardo.

The whole district was continuously inhabited from very early times,
and the Copper Age village, with imported Mycenaean pottery found
nearby at Coppa Nevigata, is well known in European archaeological
studies. The finds from this site and from Fontanarosa are now in the
small museum on the ground floor of the Municipio (next to the
Biblioteca Comunale in Piazza del Popolo) in Manfredonia, and a
reconstruction of a stratified section cut near the walls at Siponto can
be seen in the Foggia Museum.

Near to Santa Maria di Siponto is a small collection of objects from
Roman date onwards.

Venosa (ancient *Venusium*)

Venosa is a small town romantically placed on the edge of two ravines
in an ancient lake basin, on the borders of Lucania and Apulia. It has a
small museum, particularly important for its Palaeolithic material, and
some interesting buildings include a much robbed Roman amphitheatre, some Jewish catacombs of the 2nd to 6th century A.D., a
cathedral designed after the model of a French Cluniac church, a
15th-century castle and the extremely important Abbazia della Trinità.

It was here at Venosa that the distinguished Roman General,
Marcellus, was ambushed and killed by Hannibal. Livy described how
Marcellus with a small detachment of cavalry set out to reconnoitre
from a wood on a slight rise, and how Hannibal had foreseen this move
and posted his Numidian troops there to trap him. (In the Municipio
you can see an urn said to have come from Marcellus's tomb on the Via
Appia.) Hannibal himself suffered a defeat here only a few years later.

In 290 B.C. the town had been made a Roman *colonia*, the largest, in
fact, in the Roman world. But perhaps Venosa is best remembered as
the birthplace (in 65 B.C.) and the early home of the poet Horace whose
father, a tax collector, owned a small farm in the neighbourhood. Of
Horace it has been written, 'In the history of Latin literature he is
celebrated as the prince of lyric poets and as a satirist without gall, rich
in those gifts of intelligence, tolerance and sympathy signified in the
word *humanitas*.'

The Museo Briscese is in Via Vittorio Emanuele and is open from 9 to 12. It contains a lot of Palaeolithic material from the end of the second interglacial period (about 200,000 years ago). The Upper and Middle Palaeolithic finds include many Acheulean hand axes from the gravel deposits nearby, and there are more of these in the Museum at Taranto. There are also some 'Clactonian' implements of Palaeolithic date, and the third phase of that 'culture' is, in fact, called after Venosa.

The Amphitheatre near the Abbazia S.S. Trinità is of imperial Roman date and has been used as a quarry by stone robbers. Some of its stones, and those from other Roman buildings, have been built into the Abbey and into the Campanile, and the sculptured lions re-used in the public fountain near the Castle also came from the amphitheatre.

The Benedictine *Abbazia della Trinità* was founded in pre-Norman times and comprises a grandiose and fascinating structural complex. (The custodian lives near the Church of San Rocco.) On the site of an early Christian church which itself overlies a Roman temple, stands the so-called Chiesa Vecchia (unfinished, but mainly 12th–13th century). The Abbots' lodgings are to one side. Beyond this church and on the same axis lies the Chiesa Nuova. The whole building is full of French and Arab influences and incorporates many Roman details. The Campanile is one of the later elements.

3 · THE 'MURGE' OF APULIA
AND THE TARANTO AREA

Altamura, Bari, Bisceglie, Egnazia, Eraclea (at Policoro), Gioia
del Colle and Monte Sannace, Giovinazzo, Matera, Metaponto,
Molfetta, Ruvo di Puglia, Taranto, Torre Castelluccia.

This chapter describes two very diverse types of countryside, first
the greater part of the so-called 'Murge' of Apulia, with its gently
rolling hills scattered with the little white or grey conical-roofed houses
(*trulli*), particularly concentrated around Alberobello and Locorotondo,
and which peter out to the west, and secondly Taranto and the coast
immediately to the west of it, with its many rivers and torrents season-
ally pouring their alluvial deposits through the narrow coastal strip and
into the sea. These two contrasting geographical areas meet at Taranto,
west of which lay the Greek colonial towns, of which only Taranto,
Eraclea (Policoro) and Metaponto concern us in this chapter.

The 'Murge' and the Adriatic coast. This is an area which by the time of
foundation of the Greek colonies west of Taranto, corresponded with
the ancient Peucetia, the Peucetians being an amalgam of very mixed
peoples, some of whom had come from the north, others from the
west, and others from across the Adriatic and from Greece; this latter
group may have been dominant, for some of the early writers claim
that the Peucetians and other Apulian peoples were of Illyrian origin.

A number of Palaeolithic sites have been recorded, and during the
Neolithic and Bronze Ages this countryside was intensively occupied,
and its inhabitants were, at this time, in close touch with both east and
west: from the east came Mycenaean imports which, particularly concentrated around Taranto, also reached Giovinazzo and Altamura;
from the west came the practice of building megalithic tombs or
'dolmens' of the so-called Bari group (now visible at Bisceglie and
Giovinazzo) which in certain respects are similar to the French 'gallery-
graves', and which are quite distinct from the group of dolmens near
Ótranto, described in the next chapter. The Bari tombs were originally
covered with a stone cairn, and these, without excavation, cannot be
distinguished from the innumerable 'specchie' (burial cairns) which dot
the Apulian landscape. The more complex earlier examples seem to start

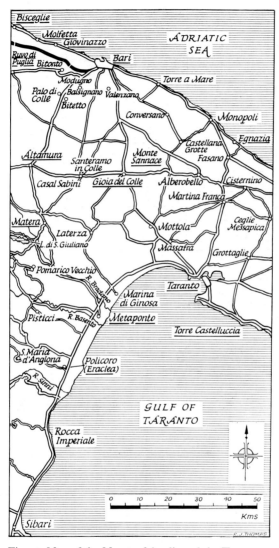

Fig. 19 Map of the Murge of Apulia and the Taranto area.

The following place names appear on the map:

Bisceglie
Molfetta
Giovinazzo
Ruvo di Puglia
Bitonto
Bari
ADRIATIC SEA
Modugno
Palo di Colle
Balsignano
Valenzano
Bitetto
Torre a Mare
Conversano
Monopoli
Castellana Grotte
Egnazia
Altamura
Santeramo in Colle
Monte Sannace
Fasano
Casal Sabini
Gioia del Colle
Alberobello
Cisternino
Martina Franca
Matera
Laterza
L. di S. Giuliano
Mottola
Ceglie Messapica
Massafra
Grottaglie
Pomarico Vecchio
R. Bradano
Taranto
Marina di Ginosa
Pisticci
R. Basento
Metaponto
Torre Castelluccia
S. Maria d'Anglona
Policoro (Eraclea)
R. Sinni
GULF OF TARANTO
Rocca Imperiale
0   10   20   30   40   50
Kms
Sibari
E. J. THOMAS

8

soon after 2000 B.C. while the small devolved versions went on being
made well into the Greek period. During this long evolution they are
found alongside Siculan rock-cut tombs in about the XVI–XII century,
and later again the pre-Villanovan urnfield cremation cemeteries at Timmari (near Matera) and Torre Castelluccia (near Taranto) reflect the
arrival of traders from the north. Out of all the ethnic strains responsible
for these various burial customs developed the more homogeneous culture of the Peucetians whose northern neighbours were the Daunians of
the Foggia district, and whose southern boundaries marched with those
of the Messapians of the Salentine peninsula. All these peoples were
sometimes collectively referred to as the Iapygians.

As we have noted, the 'specchie' were quite the commonest type of
tomb in prehistoric Apulia. They vary greatly in size, sometimes
looking like small cairns, and sometimes like collapsed castles. Some
are revetted with dry-stone walling, and some have been found to
have a standing stone on top, and their internal arrangement reflects
very different cultural influences. One of the earliest and most impressive (though recently somewhat ruined) can be visited at Giovinazzo, described on p. 127, while others are completely different both
in internal structure and in date. To mention one or two examples
only: a large one at Santa Sabina near Brindisi covered 24 rectangular
cists containing *inter alia* Mycenaean sherds and a bronze knife of
Mycenaean III B (1300–1230 B.C.) about 500 years later than the
Giovinazzo tomb had been begun. Later again another smaller 'specchia'
near Conversano contained armour and a Corinthian helmet of the
VI century, the belongings, perhaps, of some Peucetian chieftain. It is
quite common for these later tombs to contain one simple cist in the
centre of the cairn. The rock-cut tombs are less easy to find, but a group
can be seen about 9 km. to the east of Altamura on the right of the road
to Santéramo in Colle at Casal Sabini. Here there are also some 'fossa'
or trench graves belonging to the Peucetian period when the Greek
colonies were being founded on the coasts. One of the rock-cut tombs
near Altamura contained about ten skeletons and a bossed bone plaque
of a kind well known from the eastern Mediterranean, Malta etc. in the
first half of the II millennium B.C. Quite a number of the Peucetian
towns can still be identified, and remains of their town walls and houses
can be seen at Altamura, at Castiglione between Conversano (perhaps
the ancient *Norba*) and Castellana Grotte; and above all at Monte
Sannace near Gioia del Colle (see p. 126). According to their geographical position these towns gradually or rapidly absorbed the culture

of the Greek cities, particularly from Taranto, and by the time that Egnazia was founded on the borders of Peucetia and Messapia, influences from the Greek world were dominant. This and Monte Sannace are the two most worth visiting, apart from the walls and the museum at Altamura (see p. 117). Another ancient site can be explored at Pomárico Vecchio south of Matera, but the last stretch from Pomárico is hard going if not impossible by car. Many of these towns were involved in the Greco-native wars or during Hannibal's campaigns.

By the Roman period, in the late IV century B.C. the Romans, fearing the growing power of the Samnites, formed an alliance with the Iapygians, and after the year 272, when Taranto was taken by the Romans, the whole of this area fell under their dominion, and even during the Hannibalian wars the Peucetian towns were not liberated.

The Romans drove two great roads across Apulia: the earlier Via Appia, running to Taranto, further inland than the Via Traiana, built by Trajan to link Rome with Brindisi via Troia, Ruvo di Puglia and Bari. From this time onwards renewed contacts were made with the East—contacts which had begun very early in prehistoric times and which were periodically revived right down through Byzantine times, until after the Crusades, and even till today. There are few Roman remains of interest in this chapter except some buildings at Egnazia, remains of walls and an aqueduct near Rutigliano (on the road from Bari to Conversano). So many others must have been destroyed during the repeated incursions into the area after the fall of the Western Empire, and for the same reason few of the Byzantine period churches remain. There is a small, partly 6th century church at the Masseria Barsento 5 km. to the N.E. of Alberobello, and a number of small rock-cut dwellings (*laure*), many used by Basilian monks, and occasionally frescoed, are almost all that remain of pre-Norman times.

The main aspect of Apulian culture which attracts the visitor today is its architecture, particularly that of the 11th–14th centuries. (Another great moment was in the 17th–18th century with the sudden flowering of the Baroque at Lecce; that falls within the next chapter, but is outside the scope of this book.)

By the 12th century the growing commercial exchanges with the East under the Norman kings led to the building of churches and castles reflecting widely different artistic influences. On to the local restrained form of Romanesque are grafted Gothic features from France, and cupolas and decorative motifs from the Arab world, to mention the two most notable. We must remember that it was from and to Apulian ports that some Crusaders left and returned from the Holy Land. In the 13th century Frederic II left indelible marks of his personality in Apulia, and thanks to him there are still more of the impressive castles and churches already noted in the previous chapter. For 11th–14th-century buildings of special note in Apulia generally see the cathedrals, churches and castles at Altamura (cathedral), Bari, Barletta, Bisceglie, Bitetto, Bitonto (the Cathedral and Abbazia S. Leo), Conversano (cathedral, castle and San Benedetto), Gioia del Colle (castle), Molfetta, Monopoli (S. Maria Amalfitana), Palo del Colle (cathedral), Ruvo di Puglia, Trani (Ognissanti and the Duomo), Troia (cathedral), Valenzano and Balsignano, and many little rock-cut chapels and churches in the gorges below Matera and Móttola and the Cripta della Candelora and the Cripta San Marco at Massafra. (For the latter ask for the keys from the *Associazione turistica Pro Loco* in the Municipio.) Some of these have been noted in the last chapter.

Taranto and the coast to the West. West of Taranto the country changes abruptly and the rather desolate and narrow coastal strip is destined to become more and more industrialized now that malaria has been eliminated. One river or torrent after another breaks across it, depositing sands and rocks which, in the case of Sybaris (see Chapter 5), have totally obliterated one Greek city. These rivers nearly all run parallel to one another from the inland mountains of what is now known as Basilicata, but which was in ancient times called Lucania. This district, as has already been noted in the last chapter, was, like parts of Apulia described above, settled by people trading with the Mycenaean world in the II millennium B.C. and occasional contacts may have persisted until the Greeks began colonizing the coast in the VIII–VII century. For all these people coming from Greece the landscape of wooded mountains gashed by torrents flowing out through a narrow coastal plain was, as Lenormant, the French traveller and ancient historian has noted, deeply reminiscent of their own lands. He wrote: 'L'aspect du pays, la nature de la végétation, l'intensité de la lumière, tout rappelle la Grèce. Les premiers colons hellènes, en arrivant sur ces côtes, ont dû se croire encore dans leur pays.'

A road of pre-Greek date followed the shore which in early times had a slightly different alignment, and along this road were strung the many Greek colonial towns of which Taranto, Eraclea and Metaponto fall within this chapter.

Apart from the interesting chapels at Massafra and Móttola mentioned above, and the several medieval buildings of note in Taranto, this area contains little of importance. It is well worth visiting the dramatically situated church of Santa Maria d'Anglona near Eraclea (Policoro) and the castle of Rocca Imperiale, both in easily defensible positions a little inland, relatively safe from flooding and from the piratical raids to which this coast was often subjected after the fall of the Western Empire.

Museums in the area of this chapter can be visited at Bari and Taranto (by far the most important collection), Altamura, Gioia del Colle, Matera, Metaponto, Molfetta, Policoro and Ruvo di Puglia.

Altamura

The original name of this Peucetian centre is still unknown. The present town occupies the site of the ancient acropolis which once had its own defensive wall, and quite a considerable stretch of the late V century walls can be seen on the north, east and south of the town. Nearly 5 metres wide (or even more in some places) and sometimes over 4 metres high, they were constructed with big, roughly squared blocks. One might suppose that the town's name Altamura which means 'high walls' alluded to these defences, but in fact the name refers to the even more lofty ones built by Frederic II. A road is being made to follow the line of the walls outside, where, as at Manduria, there are many tombs. There are also many 'specchie' (burial cairns) in the Altamura district; most of the excavated ones have been dated by bronze objects to the VIII to V centuries.

The Museum. A new museum has recently been built in Via San-teramo, cleverly contrived on concrete stilts over an excavated area designed to remain open to view. The finds displayed include impressed wares, Bronze Age pottery of about 1600–1400 B.C., from rock-cut tombs, some VIII century bronzes, and some locally painted pottery of the VI–V century from 'fossa' graves. Perhaps the most interesting object in the Museum is one of the well-known bossed bone plaques similar to many in the eastern Mediterranean where they are often closely dated: one very like the Altamura specimen was found at Lerna in a Middle Helladic context.

The Cathedral was begun by Frederic II in about 1230 and has been added to at later dates. It contains many fine features.

Bari

The old part of Bari is pleasant and fascinating and is on the promontory around the Castle. Behind it is the newer development laid out on a rectilinear plan with few buildings of merit. The Museum is in the University in the new part close to the Central Station. (Car-parking presents a great problem and it is better to go there on foot.)

Bari's early history is not yet very clearly known, but it was certainly an important Peucetian centre at the time when the Greek colonies were still thriving along the south coast. Both Pliny and Strabo said that it was founded before the Greek colonies by Illyrians, and this belief may represent a distant echo of the contacts between the two sides of the Adriatic since the time when, in the early II millennium B.C., the earliest of the stone cairns or 'specchie' were built. In Roman times Bari became a *municipium* and later it was the chief Byzantine centre in the west, until, after many vicissitudes, Robert Guiscard conquered it for the Normans in 1071 and so brought to an end the Byzantine dominion in Italy. Its harbour was used as one of the main points of embarkation for the Crusades, and it enjoyed a period of great prosperity under Frederic II. The main annual festivity, which is well worth seeing, is the feast of San Nicola on the 7th–8th May, when most hotel accommodation is booked a long way in advance, for several days after the festa.

The Museo Archeologico is on the first floor of the Palazzo Ateneo in Piazza Umberto I in the University. (Visiting hours 9–2; closed on Mondays.) It is planned to remove it to the old town. It contains important collections from Apulia, from ancient *Daunia* (around Foggia), *Peucetia* (around Bari) and *Messapia* in the Salentine peninsula.

Entrance Hall I. Tarentine antefixes with Gorgon's or Satyrs' heads from the archaic to the Hellenistic period. Local ones from various parts of Apulia, with palmettes. Roman inscriptions, including a milestone inscribed first to the three Caesars Crispus, Licinianus and Constantinus (A.D. 317–324) and then to Julian the Apostate (361–6). Note that other milestones can be seen near the sea road of the Porto Vecchio.

Passage II. Corridor dedicated to terracotta figurines, many of which are local imitations of Tarantine ones. Notice some of the moulds used for mass production.

Passage III. Some of the finds from recent excavations, notably from rich V–IV century tombs at Monte Sannace (see p. 126) near Gioia del Colle. Red-figure ware was sometimes found in the same tombs as local geometric wares.

Passage IV. Apulian wares from various sites, again many from Monte Sannace and others from tombs at Aglie del Campo, Bari, Ruvo, Canneto etc.

Room V. Material from private collections including Messapian (VI to III century), Peucetian (VI to III century), Daunian (IV to III century) and Corinthian wares of the VII–VI century. Attic black-figure vases of the VI and red-figure of the V century. There are also early Italiot wares (late V and early IV century) including vases painted by many famous vase-painters and their followers. Campanian (IV–III century) and Gnathian wares of the same date.

Room VI. This room contains finds from one of the large III century hypogea consisting of several rooms at Canosa di Puglia (see p. 99).

Room VII. Rich Corinthian bronze armour of the VI century with a belt embossed with racing quadrigas from Noicáttaro. Other important pieces from Fiora del Colle etc. Big collection of brooches, several in silver, and small objects in gold, amber, coral etc. A few sculptured heads and reliefs.

Passage VIII. Prehistory. Palaeolithic and Neolithic finds from the Gargano. Late Neolithic wares from the Pulo di Molfetta. Bronze age wares from the Bisceglie dolmen and from a tomb at Monte Sannace etc. There is also a rich coin collection of Greek, Roman and Byzantine coins.

Other particularly important buildings in Bari are:

S. Nicola, the prototype of Romanesque architecture in the region, added to at later dates. The bishop's marble throne is probably French 12th-century work.

San Gregorio, beautiful 11th-century Romanesque church.

The Cathedral, built on the remains of an earlier one, is local Apulian Romanesque of the 12th century. It is one of the most important examples of the period. Note the magnificent illuminated *Exultet* (pre-1028) in the archives.

The Castle (open 8–1; Sundays 9–1). Part was built in the 13th century by Frederic II on earlier fortifications, and it was altered and much enlarged in the 16th century.

There is an important collection of pictures in the *Pinocoteca Provinciale*.

Bisceglie

This is a medieval town in origin and its chief interest for archaeologists lies in the dolmens which are scattered in the countryside nearby and some of which can be visited.

These Bisceglie dolmens belong to the Bari group of megalithic gallery-graves with their passages divided by septal stones like the big tomb at San Silvestro, Giovinazzo (see p. 127). Presumably of Western European parentage these tombs seem to begin much earlier than was once supposed—early in the II millennium and not far distant in date from the Ótranto group of dolmens (see p. 155).

To reach the Bisceglie dolmens, which are not very easy to find, take the road towards Corato and after 4 km. a lane with a signpost leads to the district called Chianca (1 km.) where there is one of the biggest of the dolmens. Return to the nearest road and follow it for another $2\frac{1}{2}$ km. to the hill called Cimadomo where a turning leads off (2 km.) to the dolmen called Tavolo dei Paladini. Another is in the Albarosa district not far away on the road to Ruvo di Puglia. (At least one of these dolmens is now signposted off the motorway.)

Egnazia (ancient *Gnathia*) Plate 14

This was a Greco-Messapian town later Romanized, which stood on the confines of the ancient Peucetia and Messapia. It is at Torre Egnazia, about 12 km. to the S.E. of Monopoli, on a rocky promontory, and parts of the early walls, a forum etc. of Roman date, and a stretch of the Via

Plate 14 Egnazia. General view.

Traiana can be visited. There is a custodian during normal visiting hours.

The site was first occupied in the XIII to XI centuries B.C. and then again in the Sub-Apennine period lasting down to the VI century B.C. There is, however, very little mention of it in the historical sources until the Roman period, though the walls which enclose the three sides of the town not on the sea belong to the IV–III century B.C. and may be pre-Roman. It was around this time that the well-known Gnathian ware, often ribbed, and decorated with small coloured designs on a black ground, was made here (see Plate 21B). It was once, erroneously, thought to be exclusive to Gnathia, but is now known to have been produced in a number of places.

Strabo talks of the harbour as being one of the normal ports of call for ships plying between Bari and Brindisi, and Horace, who passed through in 38 B.C. and lamented its lack of good water, enjoyed a laugh at the expense of the inhabitants who believed that incense, placed on an altar of one of the temples, ignited spontaneously.

The second period of Gnathian prosperity was during the imperial Roman period. Early in the 1st century A.D. the old mule track which Strabo had mentioned was remade and paved under Trajan, and thenceforth the land communications with Brindisi, and via Brindisi with the eastern Mediterranean, were greatly improved.

The Walls are still impressive near the acropolis on the east side of the road.

On the other side of the road the excavated area has revealed paved stretches of the Via Traiana, flanked with shops and houses, a Roman forum, a so-called 'amphitheatre', and the foundations of an early Christian church.

The shops and houses mostly belong to a relatively late date, and in some cases overlie tombs of the VI to III centuries B.C. Note that some of the smaller shops along the Via Traiana have been made by sub-dividing pre-existing houses.

The Forum is Roman and evidently overlay an earlier piazza, or possibly a temple, made with large, archaic-type blocks of stone. The wide paved area was originally surrounded by a colonnaded and roofed portico. Remains of Doric columns, capitals etc. have been found here.

The so-called 'amphitheatre' is a curious elliptical area near the Forum. It probably served for some kind of public entertainment. On the Forum side there are two doorways, and two others open into what may prove to have been the Greek agora. Originally porticos ran all around, but much of this part of the structure has been covered by later shops.

An interesting discovery nearby was a stone plinth ornamented in relief with musical instruments and a dedicatory inscription to the Magna Mater and to the goddess Syria whose cult, originating in Asia, became popular in Italy early in the imperial period. Not far away from this was found a marble head wearing a Phrygian cap, probably another god (?Attis) whose cult was often associated with the Magna Mater, so it may turn out that this area was once a sanctuary to these eastern divinities.

The tombs have produced a rich collection of vases, terracottas, and Messapian inscriptions. Some were hypogea decorated with wall-paintings, but many of the smaller tombs have now been invaded by the sea.

Eraclea *(Heraclea)* (at Policoro)

The small modern town of Policoro stands on the edge of the ancient Greek colonial site of Heraclea (see plan, Fig. 20), which, being hardly at all built over, should one day reveal its entire layout and many archaeological treasures; in the meantime the plan of the town has been partially recovered by trial excavations and air photography.

Today there is little to see, but it is worth visiting for its excellent little modern museum, and it is also on the road leading to the romantic and isolated medieval church of Santa Maria di Anglona, near Tursi, high on a bare hillside dominating the valleys of the Sinni and Agri rivers. As far as Heraclea is concerned, the plan suggests a typical urban layout of the period: the acropolis occupying one side of a town laid out on a grid system, and defended by walls. Stretches of these walls still stand to the south of the 'Castello', and here and there on the acropolis.

It was between the Agri and the Sinni (once called the Aciris and the Siris) that in 433 B.C. Heraclea was founded on the site of the earlier Siris (an Ionian colony which had been destroyed by the Sybarites in the VI century) as a joint venture on the part of the people of Taras (Taranto) and Thurii (a town not far away which had been founded by Athenians to replace Sybaris). Added to these new colonists were some

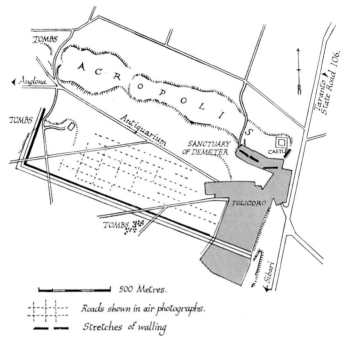

Fig. 20 Eraclea (Policoro). Plan of the town.

descendants of the Ionian colonists of Siris, still living on in the area.

The surrounding land was fertile, the town enjoyed an adequate harbour (probably at the mouth of the Sinni which is now blocked by shoals, but was navigable until the Middle Ages, and it was sufficiently near to its powerful neighbour Taras to benefit from its protection. Heraclea was designed to fill the vacuum left by the destruction both of Sybaris and Siris in the previous century. Built under the divine patronage of Heracles, it soon became a political, cultural and religious centre of some importance. It was chosen by Archytas of Taras in the IV century as the seat of the Assembly of the Italiot League which had been informed to withstand the persistent menace of the native Bruttians and Lucanians. Economically, too, Heraclea was flourishing, and at about this time it became one of the leading productive centres for early-Italiot pottery.

Politically, Heraclea's lot was always closely tied to that of Taras, and it almost surely contributed men to fight for the mother town against the Messapians and Lucanians who, in fact, succeeded in occupying it after Archidamus of Sparta (called in to help the Tarantines) had been killed at Manduria. It was liberated in 332 by Alexander, King of Epirus, who built a trenched camp to the north of Heraclea and took the town. In 279 B.C. Pyrrhus defeated the Romans with whom the Heracleans had made an alliance, near the town, but when he left to fight the Carthaginians in Sicily, Heraclea again passed into Roman hands and was evidently allowed to retain its own autonomy. In 215 Hannibal occupied the town for a short time, and the Carthaginians remained there for a few years after Taras had fallen in 212 B.C. After this we know very little. It apparently suffered greatly during the Social War of 89 B.C. when Cicero writes that all its public records were burnt. It became a Roman *municipium* in the same year, and went on being inhabited at least into imperial Roman times.

Very little can now be seen, but excavations are taking place and soon there will be more to visit. The town defences were found to have been built in the same technique as the famous Greek walls at Capo Soprano at Gela in Sicily—the lower courses with limestone blocks, and the upper ones with dried mud-bricks—and the various phases of the fortifications are now being studied. Trial excavations have also revealed not only a stratified sequence of house-foundations ranging in date from the V century to the Hellenistic period, but also a most interesting Sanctuary of Demeter and Kore, which stood outside the city bounds of Siris, but within those of Heraclea. Many ex-voto offerings from here include an Egyptian scarab, from an archaic stratum of the VII century Siris. Many of the earliest finds have an eastern, Ionian origin, which is not surprising as the colonists of Siris came from Colophon. This Sanctuary had a long life and was revered until Roman times.

The necropolis has yielded a quantity of painted pottery, and some of the early South Italian vases bear inscriptions; one shows figures which almost certainly portray the characters in the opening scene of Euripides's *Heraclidae*.

Not far from Heraclea were found the two bronze plaques known as the *Tabulae Heracleenses*, with a long inscription referring to the administrative regulations of the town, with two decrees of the late IV century concerning land belonging to two sanctuaries. On the back of one plaque was a copy of the more general law, the so-called *Lex Julia Municipalis* which was issued in 45 B.C. The *tabulae* are now in the *Museo Nazionale* in Naples.

Gioia del Colle and Monte Sannace

This little town is well placed for visiting a number of interesting places, and archaeologists may like to see the remains of an indigenous town of unknown name at Monte Sannace where recent excavations have begun to reveal considerable areas of buildings (see below).

The Museum, near the Convento di San Francesco (Piazza Plebiscito), contains a small collection of finds from the tombs of Monte Sannace, and from the Santo Molo, another settlement just outside Gioia del Colle. The objects recovered from these sites include important locally made geometric wares of the VII to III centuries, brooches, mirrors etc. There is also an exhibition of finds from various sites chosen to illustrate the cultural development of this neighbourhood from prehistoric to Roman times.

The Castle, though earlier in origin than Frederick II, was enlarged and enriched by him and became one of his favourite hunting centres.

Monte Sannace was one of the main Peucetian towns. It stands on a low rise and can be reached by branching off the 'Circonvallazione' (by-pass) for Putignano, and after about 5 km. turning left for a short distance down a lane. To avoid taking the wrong lane it is wiser at this point to ask for the 'scavi'. On one side of the lane is a little rock-strewn hill, the acropolis, and on the other side in the valley is an area of excavated houses and some defensive walls.

This town chiefly prospered between the VI and IV centuries B.C., and was abandoned a century later following the Roman conquest. The visible remains are not especially impressive. The town defences (probably late IV or III century B.C.) can be partly followed in the valley below, and some of the regular limestone blocks have got Greek letters incised on them. At one point on the south this wall stands 7 metres high. The houses in the valley, which are relatively late in date, had internal courtyards, perhaps for animals, and were probably built only shortly before the town was abandoned. As is often the case with the non-Greek towns the lay-out of the streets is occasionally rectilinear but generally rather haphazard.

The tombs, many of which are of the VI century, have often been found underlying later houses, and the crouched bodies of the dead were given rich accompaniments. Some of the known vase painters, especially the so-called 'Red Swan' painter, are thought to have had their workshops here, and the finds also include fine imported Greek wares, and amber, gold and bronze objects which are now in the museums at Gioia del Colle, Bari and Taranto. Excavations are continuing.

Giovinazzo

An important tomb has been excavated here in recent years; before the considerable spoliation to which it has been subjected, it was one of the most impressive prehistoric monuments in Apulia. It stands on the right of the road 4 km. after the level crossing on the road from the town to Terlizzi, which, from the number of standing stones in the vicinity, was evidently also a prehistoric centre.

The Giovinazzo tomb is a large cairn or 'specchia', with a dry stone revetment and a round antechamber partly made with squared stone blocks curving inwards as if to form a tholos roof; as the upper part is destroyed it is impossible to know the true nature of this structure. A rectangular aperture at a slightly higher level leads from this ante-chamber into a long, narrow burial gallery, built with slabs in the tradi-tional megalithic manner, and, like the gallery graves of Western Europe, subdivided by septal stones.

At first the excavators thought that they were dealing with a tholos tomb approached by a passage, but as the work continued they realized that this tomb incorporated a number of different influences. The long gallery, which did not reach the edge of the mound as in the true gallery graves, was in fact the burial chamber, and it was reached from a round shaft, a grandiose stone-built variant of the local proto-Apennine graves, on a more ambitious scale.

Fortunately this extremely interesting tomb can be accurately dated, as it contained among the funerary offerings Mycenaean I and II potsherds. It is thought, therefore, that it was erected for the communal burial of a family or clan in around 1800–1700 B.C., and that the latest burials were placed in it in the XVI century B.C.

If the interpretation of its excavator be accepted, this tomb seems to stand at the head of the Bari group of dolmens, all of which seem slightly different one from another, but all of which were probably gallery graves within cairns or 'specchie' belonging to various dates starting in the early II millennium B.C.

Matera

Matera, or rather the old part of it to the east, is one of the most fascinating and characteristic of the upland towns, standing high above ravines and dominated by a Romanesque cathedral. Those interested in the distant past will be rewarded by a visit to the **Museo Nationale Ridola**, while those studying the medieval period will find some extraordinary rock-cup chapels in the ravines ('*sassi*') in the countryside around the town. Here, too, is a most unusual conglomeration of rock-cut dwellings, many of the 16th century and a few still inhabited today. Until recently some 18,000 prople were living in over 3,000 caves, and these people have been re-housed thanks to the United States Counterpart Funds.

The town also has an unfinished 15th-century castle and parts of a Norman one.

Anyone wanting to do some field-work could drive to Pomárico between Matera and Pisticci. The remains of a walled Lucanian centre (Pomárico Vecchio) stand on a hill 8 km. to the S.S.E. and to find it you need to consult a large-scale map.

The Museo Nazionale Ridola (Via Ridola) (opening hours 9–12 and 3–5; Sundays 9–11).
It comprises a rich collection of Palaeolithic material from the district, with large numbers of Chellean handaxes etc. The earliest impressed and painted wares of the Neolithic period come from the Grotta Pipistrelli and other caves, and from the characteristic ditch-enclosed villages of Murgecchio, Tirlecchia and Murgia Timone, and above all from the type site of Serra d'Alto which is not far from Matera, and which was defended by no less than three concentric ditches.

The Bronze Age is represented by monochrome pottery from Murgia Timone and other sites which have also produced bronze daggers and other objects.

The finds from the Timmari urnfield, a few miles away to the west, are of particular importance, for this was one of the few so far known pre-Villanovan urnfields with cremated burials in urns accompanied by bronzes of the X–IX century B.C. (There are other finds from this site in Taranto.) There are also a number of votive terracottas from a sanctuary of Hellenistic date dedicated to Persephone, and much Lucanian and Apulian and other pottery and bronzes from the Timmari necropolis. Attic and locally produced vases from Pisticci.

The medieval churches, mostly small rock-cut chapels, can be found in the ravines (Santa Lucia alle Malve and Santa Maria de Idris in the Sasso Caveoso, and San Pietro Barisano and San Giovanni Battista in the Sasso Barisano). There are many others within easy reach of Matera.

The rock-cut villages in the 'sassi' can be reached from the Strada Panoramica dei Sassi below and to the north and east (specially south-east of the Cathedral in Piazza del Duomo).

Metaponto (*Metapontum*)

Metapontum, it is now thought, may have been founded on the site of an earlier settlement known as *Metabois*, between the rivers Bradano and the Busento; the new town was mainly Achaean in character (this has been substantiated by an inscription in the Achaean language), and its foundation in the late VIII or early VII century B.C. may have resulted from pressure on the part of the inhabitants of Sybaris who wanted a buffer state between their own city and that of Spartan *Taras* (Taranto).

Like Sybaris, Metapontum enjoyed a rich arable and fruit-growing land around and was in a convenient geographical position for cross-country trade with Posidonia (Paestum) and further north, so that in the course of time it became a flourishing commercial centre. It had one great disadvantage, however, for its proximity to the powerful city of Taranto more than offset the benefits it derived from its strong backing by the other Achaean towns of Croton and Sybaris. All of these Achaean towns would have liked to oust the Ionians from the nearby town of Siris, and in fact in 540 B.C. they united in a triple alliance, and at about this time Siris was destroyed.

By the late VI century the two temples (the one known as the Tavole Paladine and the Temple of Apollo Lycaeus described below) were set up, and at about the same time the eminent mathematician and philosopher Pythagoras transferred his school from Croton, from which he had been expelled, to Metapontum where he already had a number of followers. Here he continued to teach until he died, and his teaching continued to be respected for at least 200 years after. The site of his house was said to have been dedicated as a Temple of Demeter, and Cicero, in the I century B.C., was able to visit his tomb which was still venerated.

9

After 510 B.C., with the loss of Sybaris which was destroyed by Croton, Metapontum, deprived of its main support and ally, naturally fell increasingly within the orbit of Tarantine influence, and lost its position as a separate power in Magna Graecia; for some while little is known of its history. A battle was fought on its territory in 474 between the Tarantines and the Messapians, but Metapontum seems to have played little or no part.

By the IV century the Greek cities were more and more seriously threatened by the native Bruttians and Lucanians, and when, in 332, the Tarantines called in Alexander King of Epirus to help them, the people of Metapontum hastened to ally themselves to his cause, and Alexander had a trenched encampment near their town. After he was killed in battle he was buried at Metapontum. Thirty years later, when the campaign was being renewed by Cleonymus of Sparta, the town begged for his help against the Lucanians, but he refused the request and occupied Metapontum by force.

It is known that by the early III century the people there were living in luxury almost equal to that of Sybaris two centuries earlier, and they were proverbial for their wealth and laziness: in fact their rôle in history became less and less significant. They voluntarily gave themselves up in 278 B.C. to the Romans who were warring against Pyrrhus and the Lucanians, and they again acted from expediency when they declared for Hannibal after his victory at Cannae, and Hannibal set up a base at Metapontum from which he operated until he was defeated at the battle of Metaurus in 207 B.C. after which he removed the citizens to prevent them incurring the wrath of the Romans, and to make use of their man-power in his wars against the Bruttians. Soon after this Metapontum again fell into Roman hands, and in the course of time was made a *municipium*. All the same, Cicero, writing in the I century B.C., reported that the town was in decline, like most of the Greek cities, and by the time that Pausanias passed through, in the 2nd century A.D., nothing remained but the town walls and the theatre: the rest was completely ruined.

Air photography has revealed the approximate limits of the city walls which, grass-covered, still exist in stretches; they may have had an outside ditch. The photographs also show what appears to be a rectangular agora near a theatre and the Temple of Apollo Lycaeus (see below). The grid plan of the streets, perhaps the original layout, can be seen, as well as a large complex of buildings belonging to the artificial harbour near the mouth of the Busento.

Plate 15 The Greek temple of Tavole Paladine at Metaponto.

The Temple of the Tavole Paladine (Plate 15) lies beside the main road from Taranto to Reggio Calabria, near the Antiquarium. It is one of the best-preserved monuments of the Greek colonies on the Italian mainland. It was built in the late VI century as a sanctuary well outside the town walls, and an inscription beginning HERA . . . found inscribed on a potsherd (now in Reggio) suggests that it was dedicated to that goddess. Of its original 6 by 12 columns with archaic Doric capitals, 15 now remain, some of them still bearing signs of their original stucco. Parts of the lower course of the architrave are still in position, but we do not know exactly what the entablature was like. Some remains of the terracotta revetment are in the Antiquarium, and others in Reggio The cella seems to have been divided into two parts, one larger than the other.

The Antiquarium is a model of its kind, beautifully arranged and displayed, like the other new antiquaria in Magna Graecia. *Room I* contains plans and photographs illustrating the history and topography of Metapontum and district. Fragments of the painted terracotta revetment from the Temple of the Tavole Paladine. *Room II* houses archaeological finds from the district. Some prehistoric bronze axes found near the temple mentioned. Ionic, Corinthian, Attic black-figure wares, archaic statuettes, small ritual vases etc. There is an important series of IV century *arulae* with scenes of fighting animals etc. Coins from Metapontum, Taras, Heraclea, Croton and Thurii. At the end of the room is a reconstruction of the late VI century terracotta revetment decorations from the Temple of Apollo Lycaeus. *Room III* is dedicated to the finds from local tombs. From the archaic ones of the VI–V century are some interesting Attic black- and red-figure vases, and a specially interesting locally made VI century *stamnos* with an inscription in the Achaean alphabet. From the IV–III century tombs there is red-figure ware and pottery of the so-called Gnathian type (from Egnazia and other local South Italian potteries). In a separate case there are particularly prized objects: IV century gold earrings, pieces of silver armour, a V century gold pendant decorated with a Gorgon's head, a gold oak-leaf diadem etc.

The Museum has photographs of two important finds from Metapontum: a bronze tripod, now in the Staatliche Museum in Berlin, and a bronze helmet with silver crest in the St. Louis City Art Museum.

To reach the remains of the Temple of Apollo Lycaeus and the excavations nearby within the town area, continue westwards along the main road for a short distance, and then turn down left along road 175 passing near first a Hellenistic tomb to your right, and then a V century tomb on the left. Before reaching the station turn left, and if in difficulty ask for the Chiesa Sansone.

The Temple of Apollo Lycaeus. Excavations now taking place have revealed that this temple was built on the site of at least one earlier temple. Remains can be seen of a late VI century Doric temple. Remains of some capitals and parts of the trabeation were found here, and in Potenza Museum there are some lion-head water-spouts and fragments of painted terracotta revetments. The dedication is known from a VII century inscription on a statue of a sphinx, also in Potenza. Many VII–VI century votive statuettes have been found nearby. Excavations are continuing.

Molfetta

The old city with its splendid Duomo is chiefly of interest to archaeologists for the so-called Pulo di Molfetta (the word 'pulo' means a ravine). The sides of this limestone gorge are about 30 metres high and are perforated with Early Bronze Age dwellings; and nearby were found some hut foundations and crouched burials of Neolithic date. The name 'Molfetta' has been given to one variety of the impressed wares which were among the earliest of the wares to reach Italy from the eastern

Mediterranean and which may date from the VI–V millennium B.C. The Sicilian equivalent of Molfetta ware is called after the site of Stentinello. Molfetta has also produced some early painted wares and all these finds are in the Museum at Bari.

To reach this strangely impressive place, which is about 2 km. from the town, you should take Via V. Fornari and Via Poggioreale, passing through olive plantations until a footpath leads down into the rather overgrown 'pulo'.

Archaeologists may like to note that a small collection of finds from various Apulian sites can be visited at the *Pontificio Seminario* in Viale Pio XI.

The Duomo Vecchio stands near the sea at the tip of the old town: it is a fine, mainly 12th-century Romanesque cathedral surmounted by three cupolas—perhaps of Cypriot influence.

Ruvo di Puglia (ancient *Rhybasteinon*)

There is a lovely Romanesque cathedral here, and for those interested in archaeology, a museum, the *Museo Jatta*, containing an extremely rich collection of the local Ruvo wares for which the town was famed in antiquity. It was a Peucetian centre which reached its greatest moments of prosperity in the V to III century B.C. and one can see from the large numbers of Attic red-figure vases that the town was in close contact with Greece in the V–IV century. In the VI century most of the pottery was imported Corinthian and Attic black-figure ware, but local early-Italiot wares began to be made by the late V century, and the red-figure pottery from Ruvo is one of the first to have been made in Italy, and at the beginning of its production it was probably made by Greek potters who had settled there. As time went on, however, the local potters, who at first had remained faithful to their models, departed more and more along their own lines, and the forms became more baroque and less traditional. Examples of Ruvo wares are now to be seen in all the great museums of Europe and America.

The Museo Jatta is in Piazza Giovanni Bovio 35, and to visit this truly magnificent collection you must ask permission at the door. The collection is arranged in 5 rooms as follows: *Room I*. Mostly local Apulian wares. *Room II*. V–IV century imported Greek pottery, locally produced pottery and terracotta figurines. Note numbers 427 and 430 painted by the Italiot 'Pisticci' painter. *Room III*. V century Attic and early-Italiot wares. Number 1095 by the Amykos painter is one of the earliest local imitations of Attic pottery. Note the locally made *rhytons* made in a great variety of animal and human shapes. *Room IV*. Magnificent late V century Attic krater (No. 1501). It shows the white figure of the dying Talus (the giant bronze guardian of Crete). Bewitched by Medea (on left) he is supported by one of the Dioscuri. The fleeing woman represents the island of Crete. Above are the busts of Poseidon and Amphitrite. The ship on the left is the Argo, ready to carry Talus away. Some early-Italiot vases and IV century Apulian kraters etc. On the shelves, VI century Attic vases and VII–VI century Corinthian and Protocorinthian. *Room V*. Bronze weapons, helmets, spears etc. from the Ruvo necropolis.

Taranto (Greek *Taras*, Roman *Tarentum*)

Taranto is one of the most fascinating towns in Southern Italy. Although little remains of its ancient monuments, the charm of the splendid 11th-century Cathedral and other buildings in the old town (Città Vecchia), the attractions of its almost land-locked harbour, and the great treasures of the *Museo Nazionale* make a visit essential.

The Taranto area was frequented from very early times, and by the Bronze Age (XIV–XIII century B.C.) a number of small villages had grown up and trade relations with the Mycenaeans had been established at such places as Scoglio del Tonno, Leporano, Torre Castelluccia etc. It is not impossible that these contacts persisted uninterruptedly until the colony of Taras was founded in about 706 B.C. by Dorians from Sparta, some of whom may already have settled at *Satyrion*, the ancient site not far away at Lido Gándoli.

The site chosen for the first Greek settlement was the peninsula now occupied by the Città Vecchia—a peninsula which, like a huge natural breakwater, protected the inner harbour (Mare Piccolo) from the open sea. The eastern boundary of this first settlement was marked by a defensive wall with an external ditch whose position corresponded with the channel cut in the Middle Ages, and now spanned by a swing-bridge. Well outside the town to the east was the necropolis from which were recovered many of the great treasures now in the *Museo Nazionale*. By around the end of the V century B.C. the growing population required greater living-space, and the whole area covered by the necropolis, and now by the Città Nuova, was included within the new city bounds, delimited by a defensive wall across the peninsula. This was later to be the area of the Roman town as well.

The Greeks certainly had some preliminary clashes with the native peoples, particularly with the Messapians in the Salentine peninsula, but details of the colony's early history are very scrappy. In the course of time the Tarantines at least held, and may even have founded, the colony of *Callipolis* (Gallipoli), and there are references to their breeding cavalry horses in Messapia. Whatever may have been the initial clashes, by the mid V century Taras was able increasingly to turn its attention westwards towards the rich land around Sybaris and Siris, and to become more and more politically involved with that area. Tarantine colonists also contributed to the founding of Heraclea.

By the turn of the late V and early IV century Taras had become one of the wealthiest and most powerful Greek cities in the west, thanks primarily to its natural trading advantages, and to its fine harbour, teeming with fish including the *murex* shellfish which yielded a purple dye for colouring the locally produced woollen cloth. By the mid IV century the town was governed by Archytas, a brilliant scientist and Pythagorean philosopher who was also a shrewd politician and friend of Plato; he wisely kept on amicable terms with Dionysius of Syracuse who was campaigning along the Adriatic coast to subdue the native peoples.

Archytas had warned the Tarantines never to accept outside help, but when he had died they repeatedly ignored this advice. Time and time again throughout their history they begged help from the mother country, and eventually this habit, combined with recurrent treachery, led to their downfall.

First they called in Archidamus III, King of Sparta, to help them war against the Messapians: he was killed at Manduria. Next they turned to Alexander, King of Epirus: he campaigned widely and so successfully that the Tarantines themselves began to fear him, so they withdrew their troops and he was soon killed by treachery while fighting the Lucanians and Bruttians. Next to be called in was Cleonymus, a Spartan prince, this time against the Romans who, campaigning against the Samnites and their allies, were regarded by the Tarantines as a possible threat: once again they withdrew their support, and Cleonymus left Italy. Rome and Taras then signed a pact. By the III century B.C. the Tarantines, decadent from the effects of too luxurious living, once again begged help from outside, from Pyrrhus, King of Epirus, who landed with 25,000 men and a number of elephants. After an initial success Pyrrhus left, to fight the Carthaginians in Sicily, and after his return to Magna Graecia was defeated by the Romans in 275 at Beneventum, and went back to Greece. Taras, weakened and politically

divided, passed into Roman hands, and among the new citizens was the
first great Latin poet, Livius Andronicus.

Treachery led to the fall of the town in 212 to Hannibal who took it
from the Romans after having resourcefully carted the Tarantine ships,
which had been trapped in the Mare Piccolo, across the town to the
open sea on waggons lashed together and hauled by men and mules.
Through treachery again it was retaken by the Romans under Fabius
Maximus who so thoroughly pillaged its artistic treasures that little
survived. In these few years Rome was embellished by some of the great
works of Greek art from the two sacked towns of Syracuse and Taras;
even the colossal statue of Heracles by Lysippus was carried away to be
set up on the Capitol, but apparently his other great statue, that of
Zeus, was left.

When, in 203 B.C., Taras passed into the full sphere of Roman
dominion, it still continued to flourish for a number of centuries, and
certainly the prolongation of the Via Appia linking it with the north and
east must have revitalized the town, although, as Roman contacts grew
more intense with the eastern Mediterranean, the pre-eminence of the
famous harbour was lost to that of Brindisi.

Strabo gives a clear description of Tarentum in his day. Evidently the
town had a fine gymnasium and a spacious forum still dominated by the
huge bronze figure of Zeus. But the acropolis, between the forum and
the harbour mouth, had already been shorn of most of its former glories.
The Via Appia approached the town by a bridge across the harbour
mouth and, having crossed the present Città Vecchia and Città Nuova,
left by a gateway through the walls on the east just beyond the necropolis.

The town was still Greek in character until it was made a *municipium*
in imperial Roman times.

Museo Nazionale, Corso Umberto. Opening hours: 9.30–4 (November
1st–April 30th) and 8–1.30 and 3.30–7 (May 1st–October 31st).
After Naples this is the richest collection in Southern Italy. Although
at present the display rooms are being enlarged, the arrangement will remain as below. **The Ground Floor** will be dedicated to various districts
or regions: *Gallery A* to the ancient *Messapia* (comprising the present
provinces of Taranto, Brindisi and Lecce); *Gallery B* to ancient *Peucetia*,
province of Bari; *Gallery C* to ancient *Daunia*, province of Foggia; *Gallery
D* to *Lucania*. (A collection of inscriptions in Greek, Latin and Messapian
can be seen on request.) **The First Floor** is entirely devoted to Taranto,
from the earliest prehistoric sites until the post-Greek period. *Rooms I and*

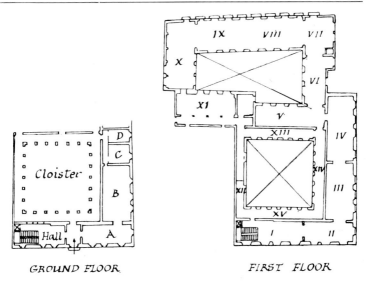

GROUND FLOOR   FIRST FLOOR

Fig. 21 Taranto. Plan of the Museum.

II Greek sculpture; *III* Roman sculpture; *IV–XI* the Taranto necropolis; subdivided as follows: *IV* painting and sculpture, *V* Protocorinthian and Corinthian pottery, *VI* native wares under Greek influence. *VII–VIII* Attic wares, *IX–X* Italiot wares, and *XI* jewellery. *Corridors XII–XV* votive terracotta statuettes. **The Second Floor** contains the prehistoric collections from the Palaeolithic to the Iron Age,

These collections are described in great detail below. See Fig. 21.

THE GROUND FLOOR

A. *Messapia.* Finds from Leporano, Manduria, Vaste, Rudiae, Egnazia (Gnathia), Ória etc. Many tombs from these sites produced local wares (often the so-called 'trozzelle' with round wheel-like ornaments on the handles) (Plate 21A), or local imitations of Greek vases together with Corinthian and Attic wares from Greece. By the IV–III century B.C. local red-figure pottery and vases of Gnathian type were being made in many different centres.

B. *Peucetia.* Important finds from Monte Sannace, Ruvo, Céglie del Campo (note two huge V century kraters with Dionysus etc.), and Canosa.

C. *Daunia*. Material from Ordona (*Herdoniae*), Ascoli Satriano and Lucera.

D. *Lucania*. Note specially Apulian pots from Roccanova, painted by the so-called Roccanova painter.

THE FIRST FLOOR (Taranto collection)

Although we know from the early writers that the town was richly endowed with fine sculptures, including two colossal bronze figures of Zeus and Heracles, made by Lysippus of Sicyon, so much looting took place after the Roman conquest in 209 B.C. that relatively little of the great patrimony of Taras is now left.

Room I. Note an unfinished archaic Kore of Ionic type from Montegranaro (VI century), and nearby another Kore of green marble; a V century head of Athena which originally wore a bronze helmet; fine mid-IV century head of Aphrodite; funerary stele with young man offering a pomegranate to the chthonic serpent.

Room II. Several fine mosaics, sculptured heads of Zeus etc. Roman copy of Hellenistic sarcophagus with Homeric scene of battle between Greeks and Trojans.

Room III. Sculptured portraits, many of imperial Roman date. Interesting Roman funerary portraits in local stone. Several 4th–5th-century mosaics.

Room IV. Mostly architectural sculpture from tombs. In the centre a painted VI century sarcophagus. Another, with pitched roof, still contains the skeleton of a great athlete of the late VI century. Note the amphorae won by him in the pan-Athenaic games. Reliefs from tombs (IV to II century) mostly showing scenes from Homeric stories. Many of these and of the painted terracottas came from the small model temples which were placed over the burial chamber. Note two big archaic figures (perhaps Victories) which were temple acroteria. Antefixes with Gorgons' heads etc.

Room V. Protocorinthian and Corinthian pottery from soon after the foundation of Taras in 708 B.C. to the mid VI century. A very rich collection with the most important pieces in the central cases.

Room VI. Corinthian and Attic black-figure wares and pottery from various Greek workshops. The Laconian wares show that the commercial links with the mother country, Sparta, were still strong; there are some beautiful cups, including one outstanding specimen painted with tunny fish and dolphins. Chalcidian amphorae, and pots from Rhodes, Chios etc.

Room VII. Black-figure Attic vases of VI century. These are particularly richly represented in the Taranto tombs.

Room VIII. More black-figure Attic wares, often painted with easily recognizable mythical and legendary scenes. The series continues with V century red-figure wares.

Rooms IX–X. Various wares made in Magna Graecia from the V century till Hellenistic and Roman times. The earliest local vase painters were probably Greeks trained in Athens who then settled in Southern Italy and painted in the local workshops set up first in Thurii in about 440 B.C., and then in Taranto around 425 B.C. After Athens was defeated in the Peloponnesian War in 404, Attic wares were no longer exported in large quantities, and local workshops in Italy developed their individual styles. Many of the favourite scenes illustrate characters from the lost plays of Euripides, or from the Orestes legends, or mythological scenes from the Trojan cycle. Some comic parodies of famous myths. A number of Apulian vases show armoured warriors with leather tunics, studded belts, high-laced boots, and tall conical helmets of a kind represented in the Lecce Museum. Others show athletes training, women preparing for marriage etc. Gnathian wares of IV–III century B.C. The red-figured wares in Southern Italy date from about 440–300 B.C.

Room XI. Perhaps the most splendid collection of jewellery in Southern Italy, with magnificent gold and silver objects made in Taranto from the VI century to the Hellenistic period, and found not only in the town but in various sites in Apulia. Note specially the characteristic diadems made of stamped gold leaf. Some magnificent necklaces, rings and earrings are in filigree or are enamelled. Note the set of gold and silver funerary jewels from a III century tomb at Canosa; this tomb produced coloured glass vessels, a jewel-case bearing the owner's name etc.

Coins from cities in Magna Graecia are also shown in this room, and note, too, the gilded fittings of a funerary bed, and a large V century bronze Poseidon from Ugento.

Corridors XII–XV. Terracotta statuettes. Again one of the richest existing collections (with over 40,000 pieces) owing to the particular development of this art in Taranto from the earliest colonial products down to those of Roman times. Some of these little statuettes, so full of grace and vitality, come from votive deposits, and others are throw-outs from kilns, or come from tombs. The earliest were made by hand, but gradually the use of moulds became more widespread. Once cast, they were retouched and embellished by hand before being coated with white and painted in bright colours. Note many figures representing dead persons heroized, or perhaps Dionysus; also many *pinakes* sacred to the Dioscuri. In the last corridor all the terracottas are Hellenistic. They often portray female figures, Aphrodite, Muses etc., sometimes dancing with swinging skirts and graceful movements. (See Plate 16.)

There is also an interesting statuette of Victory on a globe—thought to be a representation of the statue known to have been set up in Taranto by Pyrrhus after he had defeated the Romans.

This long L-shaped gallery is dedicated to prehistoric finds from the Palaeolithic to the post-Greek period. Most of the finds, which are continually being added to, come from Apulia, and some from the Gargano peninsula. Neolithic impressed or painted wares from the Grotta della Scaloria and Grotta di Occhiopinto (both near Manfredonia), Serra d'Alto, Ripoli, Grotta S. Angelo (Ostuni) etc. Considerably later are the many important finds, mostly from the Taranto district, such as Avetrana, Leporano, Torre Castelluccia etc., distinguished for their imported Mycenaean III C wares of about 1230–1025 B.C., and from Scoglio del Tonno, a headland near the present station in Taranto, which was unfortunately cut away before the days of carefully observed stratigraphy. It yielded highly interesting pre-Bronze and Bronze Age finds, including imported Mycenaean III A (about 1425–1300) and III C potsherds, and a Cretan-type dagger.

The Coppa Nevigata site near Manfredonia produced a long stratified sequence from the Neolithic onwards. Other finds from here are in Manfredonia. An extremely informative series came from the Iron Age proto-Villanovan cremation cemetery (a true urnfield) at Timmari near

Plate 16
Characteristic
terracotta figurine
from Taranto.

Matera; this yielded bronze razors, brooches etc. from the X and IX
centuries. Other sites represent the phase from the IX and VIII
centuries and the first Greek colonies. There are objects from the
Cisterna 'specchia' (burial cairn) near Lecce, and a hoard of bronzes
from Manduria.

Torre Castelluccia (ancient village)

This is reached by turning south off the Taranto–Manduria road at
San Georgio, and the village of Pulsano and the Lido Silvana Camping
site are not far away. The village which was occupied first in the Bronze
Age and then in the Iron Age and even later, is on a high rocky promontory overlooking the sea, and consists of a group of mostly rectangular
huts and part of the enclosure wall around the village. The imported

Mycenaean III C pottery reflects trade connections with the eastern Mediterranean, like so many other sites near Taranto, while other finds, bronzes and ten urns containing cremations, hint at trade connections, or even a group of settlers from northern Italy, as well. The village continued to be occupied at least into Hellenistic times, and the finds from it are in the Taranto Museum.

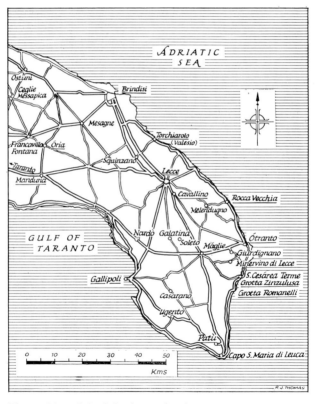

Fig. 22 Map of the Salentine peninsula.

4 · THE SALENTINE PENINSULA

Brindisi, Cavallino, Gallipoli, Grotta Romanelli and Grotta
Zinzulusa, Lecce, Manduria, Ória, Ótranto and the Terra d'Ótranto
dolmens, Patù, Rocca Vecchia, Torchiarolo.

The 'heel' of Italy is low-lying and geographically distinct from the
hillier areas to the west and north. It roughly corresponds with the
district which, in Greek times, was known as *Messapia*. Taranto is
described in Chapter 3 as it more properly belongs to the colonies of
the Ionian Coast.

Approaching it from the eastern seaways, Virgil described the peninsula as 'a low coast of dusky hills'; it is indeed undramatic country
whose chief interest lies in its rocky inlets, its many prehistoric caves,
and in the fine flowering of its Baroque architecture at Lecce. But there
are many other places of interest as well.

During the Upper Palaeolithic period many of the littoral caves were
occupied. Two of these are easily accessible to the public, and are
described below: the Grotta Romanelli with its engraved figures of
animals, and the Grotta Zinzulusa, with its unique prehistoric fauna.
Two fascinating sculptured 'Venus' figures from Paràbita may belong to
an earlier phase of the Upper Palaeolithic (perhaps around 20,000 B.C.).

Recently an extremely interesting discovery has been made at Porto
Badisco in a cave which was evidently a Neolithic Sanctuary. Not only
were there many votive offerings, but also paintings in red (early
Neolithic) and in brown or black (late Neolithic) with stylized figures
of hunters etc., somewhat like those known from Estremadura in Spain.

Being so close to the coast of Yugoslavia and Greece, this part of
Italy began very early to develop contacts with those areas, and it is not
surprising therefore to find quite a concentration of settlements on or
near the sea at such places as Taranto, Leporano, Torre Castelluccia,
Capo di Leuca etc., where pottery and other objects reflect trade relations
with the Mycenaean world between about 1400 and 1100 B.C.

Some of the tombs and so-called 'specchie' (cairns) in the Salentine
peninsula may belong to this period (the so-called Apennine period),
and a very distinctive group of dolmens and standing stones can be seen
in the neighbourhood of Ótranto, perhaps revealing evidence of connections with the western Mediterranean or with Malta. There are also

some Siculan type rock-cut tombs in southern Apulia, but the origin of these and of the 'specchie' which are commoner further north (see p. 112) are not yet known, and indeed many outside influences cannot yet be traced to their point of origin.

When the Greeks began founding their colonies along the Tyrrhenian and Ionian coasts, they did not, apparently, seriously consider colonizing the Salentine peninsula; perhaps the local Messapians (one of the so-called Iapygian peoples mentioned by Herodotus) may have been hostile: we do not yet know. These Messapians were non-Italic and may have differed from the other Southern Italian tribes in being Illyrians. It is not even certain whether Gallipoli was founded by the Greeks or only held by the Tarantines, but at some stage a Greek temple is known to have stood on the highest point of the Capo di Leuca. Co-existence rather than colonization seems to have been the Greek aim, and although strong Greek influences radiated from Taranto the native culture and language of the Messapians remained distinctive, and their walled towns at Ória, Manduria and so many other places may have been capitals of local princelings who drew their wealth from rich agricultural land and from horse-breeding. That these people were not always on amicable terms with the Greeks is shown by the fact that Archidamus, King of Sparta (called from Greece to fight for the Tarantines), met his death while besieging Manduria.

When, in due course, the peninsula fell into Roman hands, it became known as *Calabria* (a name which was much later transferred to the Calabria we know today). The great trunk road from the north was prolonged to Lecce and Ótranto, and strong cultural and commercial contacts were reopened with the eastern Mediterranean, particularly in imperial Roman times, from Brindisi.

During the Byzantine period a number of churches were built, but almost the only interesting surviving one, of that date, is the Chiesa di Casaranello (Casarano), with 5th-century mosaics, unique in Apulia. The Byzantines bitterly resisted the Normans and it is interesting to note that in the south of the peninsula the Greek rite persisted in some places till the 15th century. Frederic II, whose character dominated so much of Southern Europe in the 13th century, thought of himself always as a man of Apulia (he was crowned in the Cathedral at Brindisi), and one of his famous 'places of solace', the castle of Ória, is in the area covered by this chapter. Before his time Bohemond had built the Cathedral at Ótranto. The Gothic style is best represented in the Cathedral at Ostuni. There are other interesting churches at Galatina (S. Caterina di Alessandria) and S. Maria delle Cerrate near Squinzano. Soleto has a campanile of great beauty.

Lastly one cannot think of the Salentine peninsula without taking account of one of its most spectacular aspects: its Baroque architecture. Lavishly ornamented and strongly individual, this style found its main creative centre in Lecce which contains so many fine palazzi and churches of the 17th and 18th centuries that it must be regarded as one of the loveliest cities in Europe. Gallipoli, too, has some splendid palazzi, and the Piazza A. Salinandra at Nardò is also delightful.

Museums in the peninsula are as follows: Important collections of antiquities are at Brindisi and Lecce. Small collections are in the Castle at Ória, and in the municipio at Ugento, Gallipoli, Ostuni, Manduria and Mesagne. At Maglie there is a Palaeontological Museum in the Palazzo del Municipio.

Brindisi (Roman *Brundisium*)

Brindisi has one of the few good sheltered harbours on the Adriatic coast of Italy, and ever since the 2nd century A.D., when the immense length of the Via Appia ended triumphantly in two tall columns there, it has carried the main bulk of traffic between Southern Italy and the eastern Mediterranean. The Via Traiana also passed through on its way southwards from Benevento. Its harbour seems to have been used by the Messapians as early as the VII century B.C., but it only really assumed its primary importance with the decline of Tarentum after that town was sacked by the Romans in 209 B.C. Not only was its harbour a fine one, but Strabo, talking of its district, says, 'although there is little depth of soil, it grows good fruit, and its honey and wool are strongly recommended.'

The history of Brindisi is closely linked with Roman history generally, and it must have been one of the most cosmopolitan towns in the Roman world. In 49 B.C. Pompey was besieged there by Caesar who tried unsuccessfully to prevent his rival's fleet from slipping out by blocking the entrance of the harbour. Emperors and State functionaries departed from here or arrived from the east—men such as Marcus Aurelius, Trajan, Septimius Severus, Vespasian and, not least of these, Virgil, who died here in 19 B.C. on his return journey from Athens with Augustus. Nor should one forget Brindisi's value as a naval base for the wars with Macedonia and Greece, and in fact one of the scenes on

Trajan's Column in Rome is thought to represent the Emperor's departure from Brindisi to fight the Dacians.

Today little remains of its most ancient past except one of the lofty columns of the Via Appia. But there is also a museum, and some delightful early medieval buildings such as San Giovanni al Sepolchro, San Benedetto with its little cloister, and Santa Lucia; all these go back back to the 11th century. The Castle, originally built by Frederic II, has been added to at a later date and is not open to the public.

The Roman Columns of the Via Appia (Plate 17), erected, as said above, in the 2nd century A.D., were once a pair, but only one remains, together with the base of the other whose column was used for the Statue of S. Oronzo in Lecce. The remaining capital is of white marble, carved with the heads of Jupiter, Mars, Neptune and Pallas with 8 tritons. Probably these columns were originally surmounted by a statue. On the plinth a later inscription records the rebuilding of the town in the 10th century after it had been sacked by the Saracens.

The Museo Archeologico Provinciale is spacious and was recently rearranged. It is open from 8.30 to 12 and 3 to 6.30; holidays 9 to 12. Closed on Saturday afternoons.

A large plan of the town marks the main archaeological discoveries, and there is a reproduction of the scene on Trajan's column showing the harbour of Brindisi.

The prehistoric collections are in the *Sala Moricino* and range from the Neolithic to the Late Bronze Age, and come from caves in the Ostuni area, from huts at Francavilla Fontana, and from Siculan-type tombs at San Vito dei Normanni, and the rock-cut tomb of Cellino San Marco. Mycenaean wares of about 1300–1230 B.C. come from the latest phase of huts at Punta delle Terrare, and from the graves under the 'specchia' (or cairn) at San Sabina, which also produced late Apennine wares. There were no less than 24 rectangular graves in the cairn, whose builders were evidently strongly linked with western Greece and the Aegean. There are large situlae, cordoned pots and painted wares from Torre Guaceto etc.

The *Sala Tarentini* and *Sala Camassa* exhibit finds from Brindisi and the neighbouring district. There is much Messapian pottery and 'Gnathian' ware from Egnazia, Carovigno and Ória. Good Attic kraters of the V and IV centuries, and an Attic tazza with a painting of a

Plate 17 One of two terminal columns marking the end of the Via Appia in Brindisi.

satyr in front of a seated person; this has been interpreted as a scene of hypnotism. Some coins, inscriptions etc.

The *Sala Valesio* is dedicated to finds from an important Messapian centre (*Valentium*) at Torchiarolo, near San Pietro Vernotico. (See p. 158.) Note the ritual offerings, horse hoofs, pottery discs (perhaps for stamping votive bread), showing pincers, spades etc. Stone balls for mechanical ballistas (*onagri*).

Cavallino near Lecce (for archaeologists only)

This site offers interest only to those studying Messapian defences. The walls, originally built in the VI century, have been rebuilt at various dates until the IV century, soon after which the town seems to have been abandoned, as so far no finds of the Roman period have been recovered, though some Bronze Age occupation has been found underlying the walls. Four gates have been identified, and two of them are easily visible. A good stretch of walling with an external ditch can be found by going about 400 metres along the road which turns left at the Palazzo Castromediano, while other excavations are taking place at the end of a track, the first part of which is motorable, leading from Via Crocifisso near the church.

Gallipoli (Greek *Callipolis*)

The old part of this town, the so-called 'Città', which stands on a long rocky peninsula rather like Syracuse, does not belie its Greek name which means 'beautiful city', and it contains almost everything of interest including a castle, a rich Baroque cathedral and palaces, and the *Museo Civico*. It is well worth walking round the 'riviera' which is built on the lines of the old town walls around the point. On the mainland stands the Borgo, the new development which contains little of interest. It may have been founded by Greeks from Taranto.

The Museo Civico is in Via de Pace 108, and is open daily from 10 to 12. It has little of archaeological interest at present, but is in course of rearrangement; it has a small coin collection, a few inscribed Messapian sarcophagi, and some Greek and Messapian pottery from the sites in the tip of the Salentine peninsula.

The Fontana Ellenistica stands opposite the building of the Comando del Porto, just before reaching the main part of the 'Città'. It is a charming fountain made up of a number of elements of various dates and styles, assembled in 1560 at the latest, and re-handled in the 17th century. Three very weathered Hellenistic Greek reliefs show the metamorphoses of Dirce, Salmakis and Byblis who were turned into springs, and there are some Latin inscriptions including an epigram by Ausonius.

Within a few kilometres are two interesting small early chapels, with frescoes and Greek inscriptions; they are at the Masseria (farm) San Salvatore and San Mauro respectively, and can both be reached by turnings off the road to Lecce.

The Grotta Romanelli and the
Grotta Zinzulusa (Palaeolithic caves)

These two interesting caves open off the coast not far south of Santa Cesarea Terme, and for different reasons both are worth visiting, and both have their own considerable importance. Visiting hours about 10 till 6.

The Grotta Romanelli, a little to the north of Castro, was occupied in the Upper Palaeolithic period, and from the upper levels of the cave strata, which have been dated by radio-carbon analysis to about 10,000 B.C., came a quantity of remains of small birds and marine molluscs which must have formed an important part in the inhabitants' diet. The flint implements from Romanelli have given their name to a variant of the so-called 'Gravettian' industry. The most interesting features of the cave, however, are the figures of animals which are not only engraved on the walls, but also on loose blocks of stone—engravings which are stylistically related to groups in France and Spain. There are also some abstract geometric designs, perhaps representing very stylized human figures, and one stone was painted in red ochre. Fossil animal remains include types of elephant, hippopotamus, rhinoceros etc. from the lower levels when the climate was evidently warmer than it later became.

The Grotta Zinzulusa is only a short distance away, and it was occupied both in the Upper Palaeolithic and in the Copper Age. It is a long cave rich with stalactites, and it is particularly important to

zoologists as some of the small *Crustacea* found there are unique in
Italy, and evidently, at some very remote time, reached there from
across the Adriatic.

Visitors should enquire if the painted cave at Badisco is open to the
public.

Lecce (ancient *Lupiae*)

One of the most beautiful towns in Southern Italy, Lecce is famous for
the richly decorated 17th- and 18th-century Baroque architecture of
its many churches and its campanile. The stone, a locally quarried
golden limestone, is very soft and tractable when first cut, and then
quickly develops a hard patina, so that the buildings are hardly at all
weathered. Lecce is pleasant to stay in, and makes a good centre for
visiting the rest of the Salentine peninsula.

Lupiae, originally a Messapian town, reached its greatest prosperity
in the imperial Roman period, when the Via Traiana was prolonged
from Brindisi southwards. As mentioned above, its present glory lies
in its architecture, and its ancient remains are unspectacular. There is an
amphitheatre, and a theatre of Roman date, and an interesting museum.
Its harbour, at San Cataldo, was made by the Emperor Hadrian.

The Amphitheatre (Piazza Sant'Oronzo) is bisected by a road running
across it at a high level, so only half of it is visible. It probably belongs
to the 1st century A.D. and was built under Trajan (or possibly Hadrian).
The auditorium walls were decorated with reliefs of men armed with
swords and shields fighting lions, bears etc., or of animals fighting
between themselves; some of these are still *in situ*. There are some
inscriptions in the corridor, and various fragments of reliefs etc. are in
the *Museo Provinciale* (see below). A number of tombs (some with
Messapian inscriptions) were found near the amphitheatre, and date
from the V century B.C. to the Roman period.

The Roman Theatre (Via Arte della Cartapesta) is quite small, and
belongs to about the 2nd century A.D. Though not very spectacular,
it is fairly well preserved. The paving of the orchestra is still visible,
and so are the wide steps between it and the auditorium where the
more important spectators had their reserved seats. Some of the many
holes in the stage floor belong to a more recent date; others may have
served for the wooden scenery scaffolding.

The Museo Provinciale is in the courtyard of the Palazzo della Prefettura near Santa Croce, the richest, if not the most aesthetically satisfying of the Baroque churches. *Opening hours:* every day except Saturday and National holidays, 9.30–1; holidays, 9.30–12.30.

There is no early prehistoric material here, and most of the finds come from local sites of Messapian origin such as Rocca Vecchia (see p. 158), Rudiae and Lecce itself. There is some Greek pottery from the colonial towns, and some red-figure vases painted by known painters. Much of the more common ware was locally made, and there are a number of the so-called 'trozzelle' (with round discs on their handles), often painted with what appear to be Greek geometric designs, but in fact belonging to the IV and III centuries B.C. (Plate 22A.) Note some interesting Messapian inscriptions (one in archaic lettering of perhaps the VI century, from Carovigno, a native town which took an active part in the wars against Taranto). Also some characteristic pointed Messapian helmets in bronze, and others, for funerary use, in terracotta. In *Room II* there are some unusual doors from a III century B.C. hypogeum at **Rudiae**, painted in black and red on a white ground.

(Note that **Rudiae** itself, though just outside Lecce, is not worth visiting.)

This is not the place to describe the many splendid Baroque churches and palazzi of Lecce. But people interested in architectural styles may like to note that the church of S. Nicola e Cataldo shows a characteristic medley of influences—part is Norman, part Baroque, with an Eastern-style cupola and a Burgundian-type campanile.

Manduria

Although little of its history has come down to us, Manduria was one of the most important Messapian centres, and is well worth visiting today to see its fine ancient walls, and Pliny's Well. There is a small collection of antiquities in the Biblioteca Mario Gatti which is housed in the upper floor of the Municipio (open 9–4). (There is also an interesting bronze hoard from Manduria, with Sicilian-type axes etc., in the Taranto Museum.)

We know that Archidamus, King of Sparta, who had gone to Magna Graecia to give military aid to the Tarantines against the native Lucanians and Messapians, was killed while besieging Manduria in 338 B.C., and that subsequently, in the Second Punic War, the town, which supported Hannibal, was besieged and taken by Fabius Maximus

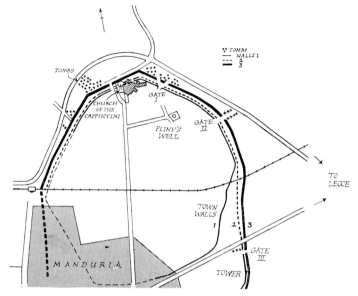

Fig. 23 Plan of Manduria.

in 209 B.C., just before he recovered Tarentum. The ancient town was destroyed by the Arabs.

Pliny's Well can be found to the north of the small town, just off the road to the Chiesa dei Cappuccini (see fig. 23). It is in the garden of a caretaker who takes you down the steps into the rock-cut grotto, a natural cave, evidently enlarged and inhabited in early Christian times, where the spring, as recorded by Pliny, keeps a constant level however much water is drawn from it.

Returning to the road and turning right you reach a fine stretch of **the ancient Walls** (Plate 18), consisting of three more or less concentric circuits of different dates. These walls can be followed round to the east for a considerable distance. **The earliest** (innermost) **wall** was made with big irregular blocks set lengthwise into the wall, and had an external ditch which was in places deliberately filled up in antiquity; this wall probably belongs to the V century B.C. **The middle wall**, near the Church of the Cappuccini, is partly built over the earlier ditch, but further east it is separated from the latter by an interval. This is a better-built wall with carefully cut ashlars, thought to belong to the IV century B.C. and to be the wall under which Archidamus was killed. Foundations of one of the wall towers have been discovered. **The latest wall** (the outermost) is very massive, sometimes about 5 metres wide, and stands to a height of over 6 metres near the Cappuccini. It had a broad external ditch. We know that these defences were put up at the time of the Hannibalian wars because they overlie or cut through some rock-cut tombs which contained Gnathian and other local wares of the full III century. These tombs, which are easily visible on the east side of the fortifications near Gate I, are arranged in groups beside the various roads leading out of the town. Over 2,000 have been identified, and while some are as early as the VI century, the majority are Hellenistic.

There is an interesting feature near Gate I where two diverging roads lead out of the town, and both at Gates I and II flights of rock-cut steps give access to the ditch.

Plate 18 The walls at Manduria.

Ória (ancient *Uria* or *Hyria*)

It is delightful to climb up from the plain of Lecce to the hill town of Ória, dominated by its huge castle built, like so many in Southern

Italy, by Frederic II, and enlarged and completed in the 14th century. Apart from a Baroque cathedral and the Castle, which houses a small collection of antiquities, and another little collection in the *Biblioteca e Museo Milizia* there is little to see today, and yet Ória had a very ancient history. Herodotus relates the legend of its Cretan foundation, and in fact the many Mycenaean finds in the neighbourhood suggest that this may have been a genuine folk-memory, albeit a little confused. Much later Ória became one of the principal Messapian towns, and was still, in Strabo's time, the seat of its reigning princes. Not very much, however, is known of its early history. Between 217 and 84 B.C. it was coining its own money, with the head of a young warrior wearing an Italic helmet—perhaps the national hero Iapygus. (The Iapygians were probably composed of several peoples of whom the Messapians were the most southerly.) During the Punic War Hannibal besieged and took the town. Later it was an important halt on the Via Appia when that great road was prolonged from Taranto to Brindisi.

The district has produced rich tombs with Messapian inscriptions, and excavations at San Cosimo just outside Ória are said to have produced Mycenaean III B stirrup-jars.

The Castle Museum. Opening hours 9–12 and 2 till dusk, every day including Sundays. It has a small local collection of Messapian pottery, inscriptions on bronze plaques, fibulae and other bronze objects.

The Biblioteca e Museo Milizia (Via P. Astore) is open from 9 to 1, and also houses a few Messapian and Greco-Roman finds.

Ótranto (ancient *Hydruntum*) and the Terra d'Ótranto dolmens

Ótranto was once much more thriving than it is today, but it is worth visiting for its 15th-century castle (the scene of Horace Walpole's book *The Castle of Otranto*), for its impressive cathedral built by Bohemond in the 11th century (it contains a remarkable mosaic floor), and for the little Byzantine church of San Pietro. Those interested in early church architecture may like to know that not many kilometres away near Giurdignana (where there are also dolmens) there is the small 8th-century *Cripta del Salvatore*.

Very little is known of the ancient history of Ótranto, but in Roman times its harbour was busily occupied with trade with the eastern

Mediterranean, and it was partly to handle this traffic that the Via Traiana was extended southwards to Ótranto. But soon its harbour was eclipsed by that of Brindisi, and it remained relatively idle until it had another burst of activity as an embarkation point for the Crusades by the Normans who had encountered particularly strong Byzantine resistance in the Ótranto district.

The Terra d'Ótranto dolmens, of which about 12 are still extant, probably date from about 2000–1500 B.C. and are thought by some scholars to belong to the Cellino San Marco culture, whose name was taken from some rock-cut tombs between Brindisi and Lecce. Though the absence of any grave-goods from the dolmens makes the problem of dating them a difficult one, it is perhaps not only a chance coincidence that some of them have pierced capstones like some in Malta, which seem to belong to the Tarxien Cemetery phase. A characteristic of the Ótranto group is that there are often associated standing stones, some nearly 3 metres tall. This group is quite distinct from the roughly

Plate 19 Dolmen in the Ótranto area.

contemporary gallery graves around Bari (see p. 112), but both may represent influence from the western Mediterranean.

The most easily visited dolmen is the so-called **Scusi** dolmen near Minervino di Lecce. (See Plate 19.) Take the road from Minervino towards Uggiano la Chiesa for about 700 metres, and you will find the dolmen on the right, among some olive trees. Slightly nearer Ótranto, but rather more difficult to find, is a group of seven dolmens and standing stones at **Giurdignano**. They are close to the farm called the Masseria Quattro Mácini which can be reached from the village, but the easiest way to get there by car is to turn towards Minervino just before reaching Palmeriggi from Ótranto. Ask soon after the turning for the farm, which lies back up a straight track to the left, a short distance along the road.

Two other dolmens worth visiting, by archaeologists only, are at **Melendugno** (half-way between Ótranto and Lecce). One, called dolmen Gurgulante, is 1 km. from the village, going towards Calimera; the dolmen Placa is less easy to locate, being further on, up a turning to the farm, Masseria lo Zuppo.

Patù

This village is not far from the tip of the Salentine peninsula. Opposite the little Church of San Giovanni is one of the most interesting tombs

Plate 20 Messapian tomb at Patù.

Plate 21A (*left*) Typical Apulian 'trozzella' from the Lecce museum.
Plate 21B (*right*) 'Gnathian' pot.

in Southern Italy—the so-called *Centopietre* (Plate 20). It is a small rectangular building with ashlar walls and a pitched roof made with long slabs of stone supported on lintels resting on several monolithic pillars, two of which have simple capitals. Two of the lintels are decorated with classical triglyph mouldings.

The building has two entrances, that on the south probably being original, while the second may have been a subsequent addition like the small window in the north wall: both the latter may have been made by the early Christians who certainly used the building and made various modifications.

On a low hill nearby was a Messapian and Roman town, and various rock-cut tombs and cists of a type thought to belong to the Messapian Iron Age once surrounded the Centopietre, and others were discovered inside, arranged at right angles to its main axis.

This monument is particularly interesting for its mixture of styles. While certainly non-Greek, there is obvious Greek influence in the use of stone ashlars and capitals, but there is also an echo of the local dolmen-type tomb which had a long history in this part of Apulia—

ranging from the Bronze Age to the time of the Greek colonies. Other tombs of this general type were once known from Vitigliano (the so-called *Cisternale*) and other sites to the south of Lecce, and some of them were underground and in certain respects reminiscent of the curious shrine found at Paestum, where only the pitched roof showed above ground. This was dated from the associated honey jars and vases to around 520 B.C. (See p. 201.)

All we can say about the Centopietre is that it is almost certainly Messapian (a Messapian inscription is said to have been found in a comparable tomb at Muro Leccese), and that it probably falls within the date-bracket of 700–250 B.C.

Rocca Vecchia

This site, near the sea, was a Messapian centre with a prehistoric level beneath part of it. It is near the 14th-century castle, and you can see a long stretch of IV–III century walls with an outer ditch, a gateway and two square towers, as well as many rectangular graves cut in the rock A number of caves along the coast here were once lived in by Basilian hermits.

Torchiarolo (near S. Pietro Vernotico)

The site of the ancient *Valentium* is hardly worth visiting except by archaeologists. The finds from there are mostly in the museum at Brindisi, but many are also in private hands. The remains of an extensive area, partly enclosed by the ancient walls, can be found to the north of the village.

5 · CALABRIA AND THE BORDERS OF LUCANIA

Capo (or Punta) Stilo (*Caulonia*), Catanzaro, Cosenza, Crotone, Locri, Papasidero and Praia a Mare, Punta Alice (*Crimisa*), Reggio di Calabria, Sybaris (near Sibari), Vibo Valentia (*Hipponium*).

As one pushes further into Calabria one is aware that the country is wilder and more sparsely populated in the central zone, though the narrow Tyrrhenian coastal strip is scattered with delightful small towns and villages such as Paola, Tropea and Scilla (later thought to be the Scylla of Scylla and Charybdis in the *Odyssey*). The Ionian coast is more deserted but is rapidly becoming attractive to the tourist since the building of the great motorways, the *Autostrada del Sole* and the Potenza–Metaponto road, has made it more accessible.

Calabria is dominated by two high massifs, both of which, in autumn, are liable to torrential downpours and landslides which make the tortuous roads dangerous: the Sila in the north (almost Alpine in character, and ideal for camping), and in the south the less hospitable Aspromonte with its magnificent views across to Sicily. The Sila is a granite plateau, studded with lakes, and is delimited on the north by the river Crati, rising near Cosenza and flowing first northwards and then eastwards to its mouth in the vast alluvial plain of Sybaris, under which lies buried perhaps the most opulent of all the western Greek colonies.

Upper Palaeolithic caves can be visited at Praia a Mare, and not far away at Papasidero, and a long series of Neolithic and Copper Age sites have produced finds which appear to correspond with the sequence established for the Aeolian Islands. By the Bronze Age the picture is less clear; so far there is not the same evidence for contacts with the Mycenaean world which are so noticeable around Taranto and the Salentine peninsula, but in the XV–XIII centuries B.C. the Apennine Culture seems to have flourished, and to have lingered on later than in some parts of Italy. By the Later Bronze Age and Early Iron Age (XIII–VIII centuries) Southern Italy was inhabited *inter alia* by so-called Siculan peoples akin to those in Sicily, and their rock-cut tombs, often in large cemeteries, can be seen at Ianchina and Canale, above Locri, at Calanna near Reggio Calabria, and elsewhere.

By now different tribes were beginning to be distinguishable, and

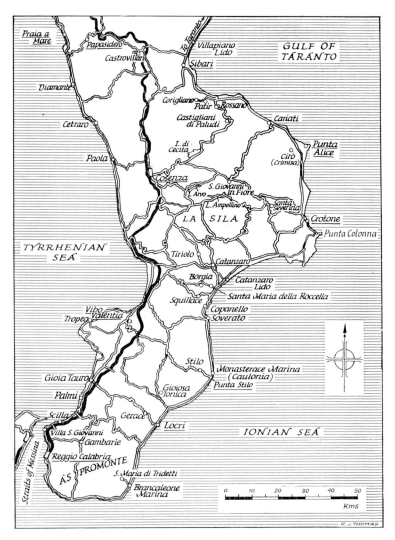

Fig. 24 Map of Calabria and the borders of Lucania.

one of them, the Ausonian tribe, was responsible for the invasion of Lipari in about 1250 B.C. To these people must probably be attributed the so-called 'fossa' or trench graves, often, too, found in extensive cemeteries such as Torre Galli near Tropea. Later a new burial rite, cremation, also found at Tropea and a few other sites, points to at least sporadic coastal settlement by so-called proto-Villanovan people, but so far they have left only a few traces as far south as Calabria.

These various peoples whom the Greeks encountered when they began to establish colonies along the south and west coasts had gradually, as time went on, become less distinct one from another, and had become referred to collectively as Bruttians—Calabria being called *Bruttia* until the Byzantine period.

The Greeks established colonies and sub-colonies at a number of places described in this chapter—Rhegion (Reggio Calabria), Locri, Crotone, Hipponium (Vibo Valentia), Caulonia, Sybaris etc.—and several of these were famed for their artistic achievement and for their many great philosophers, doctors, sculptors, writers and athletes who lived in them and had a profound influence throughout the Greek world. The Bruttians and their neighbours the Lucanians lived mostly in inland settlements which, according to their proximity to the Greek cities, became more or less Hellenized. Often their hill villages and towns are difficult of access, but one can be found on the borders of Bruttia and Lucania at Castiglione di Paludi, near Rossano. As time passed the Bruttians grew stronger and more closely united, with their capital at Cosenza, and they became such a menace to the Greeks that sometimes outside help (for instance from Dionysius the Great of Syracuse and, later, from Pyrrhus) had to be called in against them. Soon, too, the Romans were spreading their influence southwards, eager to enjoy the spoils of the rich and culturally advanced Greek cities. At first they wisely tried to assimilate the Bruttians, but their ambition was delayed during the Second Punic War, against Hannibal, and it was only achieved after his withdrawal.

The Romans have not left many monuments to see in Calabria, but there is a small theatre at Gioiosa Ionica, an interesting building, perhaps also a theatre, at the Parco del Cavallo site overlying ancient Sybaris, and the newly excavated theatre and amphitheatre at Borgia, the Roman *Scolacium*. Roman influence can also be seen in the theatre at Locri. In about 132 B.C. the Via Popilia, the long coast road down to Reggio from Capua, was built.

Gradually the new *coloniae* and other Roman and native settlements
11

took the place of the once Greek cities. Under the Romans both the economic and social life of the Region (it was Region III of Augustus), and its religious life, by now an amalgam of Italic, Greek and Roman concepts, grew steadily more coherent, and in time accepted the Christian faith.

When the Western Roman Empire came to its end in the late 5th century the Byzantine domination of the Eastern Empire held on precariously in Calabria, and in spite of the short Visigothic invasion in the 6th century, of pressure during the 7th century from the Langobards who succeeded in reaching as far south as Cosenza, and of sporadic Arab raids in the 9th century, Calabria remained a stronghold of Byzantine influence until it fell into Norman hands in the 11th century.

In the 6th century Calabria was distinguished for its rôle in keeping the light of learning from being extinguished in much of the peninsula, and in this regard Cassiodorus must be the first to be remembered. Author of the *History of the Goths* and other learned works, he set up his rich library at the Monasterium Vivariense at Squillace. At about the same time one of the most perfect and ancient of the illuminated Gospels in the Greek language, the *Codex Rossanensis*, was produced at Rossano, where it can still be seen. (Rossano was later to become the home of St. Nilus, a Basilian monk and one of the most eminent men of the 10th century.)

The Byzantine domination was able to reassert itself in the 10th century, and many monastic settlements of Eastern origin were founded, often by followers of St. Basil of Caesarea. Several small and highly interesting churches belong to this period, notably the 'Cattolica' at Stilo, San Marco at Rossano, and the Baptistery of Santa Severina, all in the hills a little inland as the coast was now dangerous because of the piratical raids to which it was subjected and the malaria infesting its partly silted river mouths.

By the 11th century the Normans pushed westwards from Apulia and conquered Calabria. To this period and to the following two centuries belong some most interesting buildings including those at Gerace, Santa Maria di Tridetti near Brancaleone Superiore, Santa Maria della Roccella near Catanzaro, Santa Maria del Patir near Castiglione, the Cathedral at Tropea, the Cathedral and small church of San Francesco di Assisi at Cosenza, and the Badia Florense at S. Giovanni in Fiore.

Museums. There is the splendid and recently enlarged and modernized *Museo Nazionale* at Reggio Calabria, the most important in Calabria.

Modern *antiquaria* are at Locri, Sibari and Crotone, and smaller collections at Catanzaro, Vibo Valentia, Cosenza, and in the *Biblioteca Comunale* at Castrovillari. Tropea has a collection of early Christian epigraphy in the Palazzo Teraldo, and at Palmi there is the small but interesting *Museo Calabrese di Etnologia e Folclore* in which it is possible to see wooden spindles, and pottery masks with their tongues stuck out against the evil eye etc. which, although mostly dating from the last century, are almost identical in design and decoration to ancient Greek and Punic ones—marking an unbroken tradition.

Capo (or Punta) **Stilo**, near Monasterace Marina (site of Greek town of *Caulonia*), and **Stilo** (Byzantine church)

This was the site of the Achaean colony of Caulonia which should not be searched for near the modern town of that name some kilometres away. There are remains of the curtain walls of the town, and the foundations of a large Doric temple. A short distance away inland is one of the most fascinating churches in Calabria, the little 10th-century Byzantine 'Cattolica' at Stilo (see below).

The colony was founded in the VII century, but was never very large, and as time went on it found itself uncomfortably wedged between two much more powerful neighbours, Croton and Locri. Apart from a peaceful period in the V century, when the Pythagorean sect had a big following in Caulonia, its history was continually a tormented one, like that of so many other Greek cities. It was destroyed in 389 B.C. by Dionysius of Syracuse who handed over its territory to his allies the Locrians, who may have repopulated it soon after; it was again destroyed during Pyrrhus's campaigns in Magna Graecia. Both these men were campaigning for the Greek cities against the native peoples. Again Caulonia grew up, but was then occupied by Hannibal who may have removed all its inhabitants. By Strabo's time it was completely ruined and deserted, and Pliny referred to it as *vestigia oppidi*.

The town walls and the temple foundations can be seen at Capo Stilo, a few minutes' walk from Monasterace Marina. Follow the Taranto road and turn right, down some steps before crossing the railway.

The walls are unique in that they are not made in the usual Greek manner with blocks of stone, but with large water-worn pebbles collected from the river bed and held together with a sort of cement made with greasy earth.

Only parts of the stylobate of **the Temple** remain, as this was first ruined by an earthquake, and then, later, its columns were smashed up for lime. It was a large, early V century Doric building, and its dedication is uncertain, though it may have been to Apollo Katharsios. Parts of its cornice and rain-water spouts are in the museum at Reggio Calabria, and in the same museum are some fine polychrome terracotta fragments from the revetments of another, smaller temple some distance away.

The little church of *the 'Cattolica'* a few miles inland at **Stilo** is completely Byzantine in style, and is surmounted by five tiled cupolas. It belongs to the 10th century like the Church of San Marco further towards Taranto at Rossano (see p. 162). Both of these small brick-built churches would be perfectly at home in Greece or Armenia, and it is a delightful surprise to find them in Calabria.

(To visit the *'Cattolica'* ask for the Sacristan of the Duomo.)

Catanzaro

Spectacularly sited on a long hill, Catanzaro is probably not worth visiting except by archaeologists wanting to see the Museum. It is not, apparently, a very ancient town, probably not earlier than the Byzantine period (9th or 10th century). Its name comes from *Katantzarion* (*Kata*, under, and *antzarion*, terrace) referring to the terraced slopes in the valleys around.

The Museo Provinciale (near the entrance to the gardens of Villa Trieste, at the southern end of the town) is awaiting new premises. It contains a very mixed collection including stone implements from Neolithic and later sites in Calabria and other parts of Italy; Greek pottery; a fine V century Greek helmet from Tiriolo, embossed with great delicacy; Roman objects, and a rich collection of Greek, Roman and post-Roman coins. (Among the pictures there is a Madonna and Child by Antonello da Messina, perhaps the greatest of the South Italian painters of the Renaissance. Note that there are two others in Reggio Calabria and one in Paola on the Tyrrhenian coast not far from Cosenza.)

Not far from Catanzaro Lido, just off the state road 384 leading to Borgia, is the large ruined 11th-century Church of Santa Maria della Roccella, one of the most notable in Calabria.

Cosenza (Roman *Consentia*)

Built on a hill above the junction of the Crati and Busento rivers, this was probably originally a Bruttian settlement, for it was described by Strabo as 'the metropolis of the Bruttians'. Although it was later Hellenized, its history was undistinguished in antiquity. When Alexander, King of Epirus, came to Magna Graecia at the request of the Tarantines to fight against the non-Greek peoples, he is said to have been defeated by the Lucanians near Cosenza, and buried there. During the war against the Carthaginians the town stood out for Hannibal, but after 204 B.C. it was definitively in the hands of the Romans, under whom it thrived. Both Varro and Pliny praised its excellent wine and fruit, specially its figs, and by imperial times it was an important halt on the Via Popilia. According to one tradition, it was here that Alaric, King of the Visigoths, died, and he was buried in the bed of the river Busento in 410 together with all the treasure he had looted from Rome.

Today Cosenza is mainly visited by those wanting to spend some time exploring the uplands of the nearby Sila. The old part of the town has some charm, and some interesting buildings including the small Church of San Francesco d'Assisi and its cloisters. The Cathedral, which was consecrated in the presence of Frederic II, is over-restored.

The Museum is in the Villa Communale in the corner of Piazza XV Marzo. The most interesting finds displayed here come from the VIII–VII century necropolis of *Torre Mordillo*, near Spezzano Albanese, a miscellaneous collection of pottery, bronze swords, brooches, armlets etc. from a ransacked group of about 1,000 'fossa' or trench graves; the inhabitants of the nearby settlement were not very closely in touch with the Greek colonies, but received a little pottery from them.

From *Francavilla Marittima*, once thought to be the site of *Lagaria*, there are bronzes and pottery of the VIII–VII century. There was a Sanctuary of Athena at this site, and from it came an inscription on bronze dedicated to the goddess by an athlete to celebrate his victories in the Olympic games. Some other finds from this site are in the *Antiquarium* at Sibari. The Cosenza Museum also has bronzes from Michelicchio (Cerchiara) etc.

Crotone

Not a particularly attractive town today, in spite of a charming quarter around the Castle and Museum, Crotone is worth visiting for two main reasons. Its great past as one of the major cities of Magna Graecia and home of Pythagoras and his school is well evoked in the small new Museum, and the Sanctuary of Hera Lacinia, on a promontory a few kilometres away, even if only one column remains today, is still (if seen at the right time when few people are about) one of the most moving places in the Greek West.

The town was founded, probably by Achaeans, in about 708 B.C. only a year or two before the foundation of Taranto. The acropolis was on the hill now occupied by the Castle, and by Livy's time, at least, the town walls had a circuit of about 20 km. We do not know exactly how extensive the Greek walls may have been, but we can say that, at the moment of its greatest political and territorial expansion, its lands probably stretched across to the Tyrrhenian Sea. Its harbour at the river mouth, though only small, was evidently sufficiently equipped, by the time of Dionysius the Great, to contribute 60 warships.

The growing power of Croton by the early VI century caused alarm among the neighbouring Locrians, and clashes were sometimes recorded; these do not seem to have affected the steady rise in the town's prosperity. In about 540 B.C. the great Pythagoras settled there, and his influence spread throughout the Greek world. Remembered by most people today for his geometrical theorem, Pythagoras was mainly a philosopher who based his beliefs on the theory of the transmigration of souls—a theory which was to be lightly ridiculed by Shakespeare in *Twelfth Night*. (*Clown:* 'What is the opinion of Pythagoras concerning wildfowl?'—*Malvolio:* 'That the soul of our grandam might haply inhabit a bird.') Pythagoras also attempted to apply some of his philosophical ideals to the problems of local government, but as time went on his teaching was regarded as insufficiently democratic; he and his followers were driven out and his doctrine only lingered on in an attenuated form. Pythagoras, however, was not the only man of renown in Croton during the VI century. Alcmaeon (said to have been the first man to write a treatise on anatomy) and Democedes, one of the first distinguished surgeons, both added to the fame of the Greek medical world. Moreover the men of Croton were famed for their prowess as athletes, and the greatest of these was Milo, a follower of Pythagoras, a man of prodigious strength who was chosen to lead Croton in about

510 B.C. in its major war against Sybaris which, as is well known, was totally obliterated. It is also known that on another occasion, in one of the Olympic contests, the first seven places in the race were won by men from Croton.

After the successful war against Sybaris there followed a long period when Croton enjoyed wide political and territorial dominion, but eventually excessive good living seems to have brought about a certain decadence. By now the native Lucanians were pressing southwards and menacing the Greek towns, many of which, including Croton, formed themselves into a league. But their policy was confounded by Dionysius of Syracuse who crossed into Magna Graecia and made an alliance with the Lucanians in an attempt to take Rhegion (Reggio Calabria) and so be able to dominate the Messina straits. During the campaign he took Croton in 379, and held it for some years, but less than a century later the town was again threatened, this time by Lucanians and by Bruttians from the area now called Calabria. These people besieged Croton, and it was then taken by Agathocles of Syracuse who used it as an operational base in 299. Again Croton was badly damaged during the period of Pyrrhus's campaign in aid of the Greek cities, and Pyrrhus himself occupied the town for a short time. But in 277 B.C. Croton fell to the Romans, and according to Livy the city was thenceforth reduced in size. Even then its troubles were not over. During the war between the Romans, and the Carthaginians under Hannibal, the town temporarily fell into the hands of the Bruttians and Carthaginians fighting together, and Hannibal used Croton as one of his naval bases. It was in fact from here that, having been driven further and further south and increasingly restricted in his area of domination, Hannibal sailed for Africa, having first set up an inscription recording his military exploits in the nearby Sanctuary of Hera Lacinia.

The Museum is near the Castle in Via Risorgimento. *Opening hours:* weekdays, except Mondays, 9.30–4; Sundays and holidays, 9.30–1.30. Beautifully arranged like the other new museums on the Ionian coast (Locri, Eraclea, Metaponto), it houses prehistoric, Greek and Roman finds from the district and from the area of Croton's domination, as well as from the Sanctuary of Hera Lacinia.

Ground floor. Many of the prehistoric finds come from old collections now brought together for the first time. There are a few Neolithic implements from the Catanzaro district, and a number of bronze brooches etc., some of which may have come from the *Torre Mordillo* (see p. 165) necropolis. There is also a good representative collection of coins from the various cities of Magna Graecia down to imperial Roman times. The earliest coins struck in Croton itself belong to the mid VI century. Other cases on this floor are devoted to a chronological arrangement of votive terracottas. *First floor.* Dedicated almost wholly to the area of Crotone and the Sanctuary of Hera Lacinia at Capo Colonna (see below). Some small bronze figures of non-Greek manufacture reflect the occupation of Croton by the Bruttians in the III and II centuries B.C. A number of interesting finds from the Sanctuary of Hera Lacinia. There is also a display of Greek and native wares from unknown provenances, chosen to illustrate the chronological sequence of the imported pottery and of the local schools of pottery making which grew up. Finds from Cirò (the ancient *Crimisa*) and from Monasterace Marina (*Caulonia*), both of which towns were under the dominion of Croton. A few objects come from the Sybaris district and from Metaponto. *Cellar.* Various large architectural fragments.

The Sanctuary of Hera Lacinia at Capo Colonna (Plate 22). (To reach this you leave Crotone by Via Cristofero Colombo and Via Poggioreale, and follow the coast road for about 11 km.) It is worth trying to visit this temple early in the morning or towards sunset, and although it is disappointing to see only one of the original 48 columns still standing (there were many more until the 16th century), we know so much about this deeply venerated place that a little imagination may help us to visualize and re-people it.

The cult of Hera Lacinia was begun here in the mid VI century (there is an inscription of that date, written in the Achaean alphabet, in the museum at Crotone) and it lasted at least until the 2nd century A.D. Practically nothing of the earliest building on the site survives, but part of its *sima* was discovered, and a few votive objects which go back to the VI century. The building to which the single column belongs was set up in the first half of the V century, and soon became the national sanctuary of the Greeks in Magna Graecia, annually celebrated with processions and assemblies in honour of the goddess. This lonely column standing on the rocky promontory within sound of the waves, was once part of the most splendid Doric temple in Southern Italy. It originally had 16 side columns and a double row of columns along the front; the frieze was decorated with Parian marble sculptures, and the magnificence of its white marble roof tiles was renowned in ancient

Plate 22 Capo Colonna (Crotone). View of Sanctuary of Hera Lacinia.

times. Inside there were many treasures: a massive gold votive column, paintings by the celebrated artist Zeuxis, including a portrait of Helen of Troy painted from a model chosen from the most beautiful girls of Croton, and statues of Olympic victors. When Hannibal left Magna Graecia, he set up a large bronze plaque here, inscribed in Greek and Carthaginian to commemorate his many military exploits. It was only very impious men who had the audacity to rob such a treasury. Dionysius, 'cruel, vindictive, and a profane plunderer of temples', lived up to his reputation and despoiled it. Hannibal, too, was tempted to rob it, but probably refrained, and at a later date still Pompey robbed it, though it had already been desecrated and its marble tiles stripped off for re-use in Rome.

In Roman times, at least, the temple stood in a walled *temenos* or sacred area, and part of the enclosure wall that can be seen today is clearly of Roman build. Livy described it in these words: 'Six miles from the famous city was a temple more famous than the city itself, that of Lacinian Juno, revered by all the surrounding peoples. There a sacred grove, which was enclosed in dense woods and tall fir trees, had in its centre luxuriant pastures where all kinds of cattle, being sacred to the goddess, could pasture without any shepherd.'

It is improbable that it was so hidden that sailors in coasting ships could not have glimpsed it, brilliant white in the daylight and glowing pink at sunset, and offered up a prayer to Hera Lacinia as they passed. We know from the *Aeneid* (Book III) that sailors set their course from temple to temple along the Ionian coast.

Locri (*Locri Epizephyrii*) Fig. 25

This site, near the sea in a delightful countryside, can easily be reached in an excursion from Reggio Calabria, together with the impressive Cathedral at Gerace a few miles inland, partly built with columns from the ancient Locri. *To visit:* The Antiquarium, the town walls, the Temple of Marasà, the theatre, and the *Centocamere*.

When, in the first half of the VII century, Locri was founded by Greeks from central Greece, Euboea and some of the islands, they found that the most desirable sites for colonizing had already been taken. First the Locrians tried to settle on Capo Zephirio nearby, but soon afterwards they transferred to the present site which had evidently been inhabited by native 'Siculan' people for some centuries, since their rock-cut tombs of the IX to early VII century B.C. have been found close by at Canale and Ianchina a little inland.

Certainly the site had not much to offer: only a narrow coastal plain and a harbour which can never have amounted to anything considerable (changes in the shore line have obliterated it, but it was probably at the mouth of the Portigliolo torrent). But it was conveniently placed for three reasons: it lay on the ancient east-west coast road (which, bisecting the site of Locri, is still known as the 'dromos'), its communication routes with the Tyrrhenian coast via Taurianova were relatively easy, and it was the last port of call for westbound ships plying to Sicily.

The city, whose remains now lie buried below olive groves sloping towards the sea, and a small modern hamlet strung out along the 'dromo', never had a real and proper acropolis: instead it was domi-nated by three heights or citadels (Castellace, Portigliolo and Man-nella). Since the produce from the cultivable land between the steep hills and the sea can never have been more than adequate for their own needs, the Locrians had to depend for their wealth on their manufactured goods, and they soon started to make pottery, bronze objects (particu-

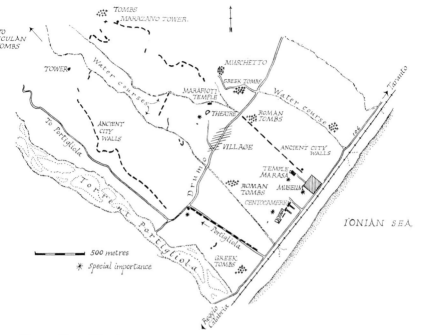

Fig. 25 Plan of Locri.

larly mirrors), terracotta revetments for temples etc., and sculpture of a
very high and individual character—individual, perhaps, owing to their
contacts with the indigenous people and with mainland Greeks, and
Ionians, more of whom arrived around 500 B.C. Two great masterpieces
of local art, the so-called Ludovisi and Boston thrones (the former is
now in the Terme Museum in Rome) (see Plate 25), were both found in
Rome, but are thought to have been looted from the Locrian Sanctuary
of Persephone. Another fine work is the acroterion of the Dioscuri
(Castor and Pollux) found at the Marasà temple and now removed to
Reggio Calabria from Naples. Famous, too, as locally produced works
of art are the exquisite small terracotta plaques depicting scenes in the
life of Persephone (now mostly in Reggio and Taranto and described on
pp. 181–182).

The history of Locri was dominated by fear of its Achaean neighbours Sybaris and Croton on the one hand and Rhegion (Reggio
Calabria) on the other, for Rhegion, generally in bitter enmity with

Locri, and envied by all for its advantageous position on the straits, always had to act with expediency, switching its alliances to best serve its immediate needs. It is doubtful if Locri would have survived these difficulties had it not been for the help sent from Syracuse, its ally from the time of Hieron I; indeed Locri was again and again used as a bridgehead for Syracusan interference in Magna Graecia. Help, too, sometimes came from Taranto or even Sparta.

Locri seems generally to have been well governed, and soon after its foundation it had, under Zaleucus, the earliest written code of laws of any Greek state. Its religious life, centred in Persephone, was soon active, and the great Sanctuary of the goddess, and the first temple at Marasà, belong to the years soon after the foundation.

Fortunately Locri is almost entirely free of modern development, so that there is every chance that in future years excavation will yield a great deal of information about its life and buildings. For the moment what we know of its history largely comes from the written sources. Some time, probably in the mid VI century, Locri, fighting in alliance with Rhegion, won a decisive battle against Croton at the river Sagras, and it was at about the same time as this that Locri founded its new colonies at Medma, Metaurus and Hipponium on the Tyrrhenian coast, and several other unidentified colonies as well. In 493 B.C. another contingent of Ionians, from Samos, took refuge in Locri, adding to the already existing Ionian influences in its art and architecture. Locri was a flourishing artistic centre by now, and was also regarded as such a model of intelligent government that Pindar sang its praises in one of his Odes.

Always faithful to its alliance with Syracuse, Locri refused permission to the Athenian fleet to anchor off its coasts when the Athenian invasion of its ally was imminent in 415 B.C., and shortly after this the link between the two towns was still further strengthened by the marriage between Dionysius the Great and a Locrian girl. When Dionysius was fighting in Magna Graecia, he handed over the territory of Caulonia to the Locrians after that town had been destroyed in 389.

After the death of Dionysius a change for the worse took place, for his successor Dionysius II, driven out of Syracuse, took refuge in Locri which he governed so disastrously that soon steps had to be taken to get rid of him. A thoroughly degenerate man, he held bizarre orgies, some of which are described in colourful terms by Strabo. 'He used to sneak into the bedchambers of the girls going to be married, and then let loose doves with cropped wings upon them in the midst of the banquets and make the girls dance round naked.' To make the matter even more ludicrous the girls chasing the doves were provided with odd pairs of sandals with one high and one low heel, 'all for the sheer indecency of it'. Naturally it was imperative to remove this colourful figure from the scene, and one of the leading protagonists in doing so was the Pythagorean philosopher Echecrates. His plot was discovered and he was saved only through the intervention of Plato who, it is interesting to find, immortalized Echecrates by giving him the part of interlocutor in the *Phaedo* (the famous dialogue concerning the death of Socrates).

By now the whole of Magna Graecia was under pressure from the native peoples, in the case of Locri, from the Bruttians, who cast covetous eyes on the rich cities of the Greeks. At the same time, in the III century B.C. these cities were often on hostile terms with the Romans, now actively spreading their sphere of interest throughout Southern Italy. Early in the century the Tarantines called for the help of Pyrrhus, King of Epirus, against the Romans and natives, and Pyrrhus put a garrison at Locri. Apparently his soldiers so misbehaved themselves that the Locrians drove them out and this so incensed Pyrrhus that, according to an account by Livy, he 'robbed the Treasury of Persephone . . . and loaded his ships with stolen money while he himself marched away by land. Next day his fleet was battered by a terrible tempest, and all the ships laden with sacred money in their holds were driven ashore.' Pyrrhus, deeply alarmed, gave orders for the treasure to be restored. This occurrence has recently been verified by the discovery of the temple archives inscribed on bronze tablets.

After this the Locrians submitted to the Romans until the Second Punic War when, thinking that they would be better off allied to Hannibal after his victory at Cannae in 216 B.C., they switched their allegiance. A few years later their town was being besieged by the Romans with great violence when Hannibal sent his Numidian cavalry to its relief, and these men 'caused such terror among the Romans that they fled pell-mell into the sea and ships, leaving their siege-works and engines with which they were battering the walls'. Not long after this the town was recaptured by the Roman Scipio Africanus, and his legate not only plundered the Sanctuary of Persephone but so ill-treated the inhabitants that they complained to the Senate who granted them liberty and the right to make their own laws.

Little more is known of Locri: it almost surely diminished gradually in size and importance until it was wiped out by the Arabs, and its remaining inhabitants fled inland into the hills to Gerace.

The Antiquarium is on the north side of the Reggio–Taranto road, and is laid out with clear plans and photographs illustrating the history and artistic development of Locri. These newly built antiquaria are models of their kind, and fascinating to the layman as well as the archaeologist. The collection includes much important local material with pottery and bronzes from both the pre-Greek and Greek tombs, architectural fragments from the temples, votive offerings from the Sanctuary of Persephone and Grotta Caruso, Roman inscriptions, and coins from Locri and other Greek cities. The richest remains from the site are housed in the impressive new rooms in the *Museo Nazionale* at Reggio Calabria (see pp. 180–182).

The Walls. Much of the town wall can still be traced today but the visible stretches seem to be as late as the III century B.C. The only traces of the earlier wall are at *Centocamere* and another point. The late wall was interspersed with round and square towers, many of which can be seen. There must have been gateways at each end of the 'dromo' and there were others to the north and towards the sea. Some of the best-preserved walls are marked with an asterisk on the plan (Fig. 25).

The Temple of Marasà. The remains of this important temple, now thought to have been dedicated to Zeus, can be found a short way behind the Antiquarium. First built in the VII century, it had a long cella divided into two naves, and it was faced with terracotta slabs bearing a painted meander design. In the VI century a surrounding colonnade of stone was added, and many architectural terracottas belong to this period. In the latter part of the V century this temple was replaced by a larger and more splendid one, built in the Ionic style on a slightly different orientation. It was unusually long with 17 side columns and it consisted of a cella, pronaos and opisthodomus. Part of one column remains. Some of the elements from this temple (stone lion-head spouts, fragments of marble acroteria etc.) may belong to the IV century. The main central acroterion depicted a Nereid flanked by Dioscuri on horseback, supported by Tritons. As is mentioned above this is now in the Museum at Reggio Calabria. A big altar is still visible in front of the temple, but much of the structure is very ruined. The design of the remaining Ionic column base can be compared with some from Samos.

Plate 23 Locri. Acroterion from the Temple of Marafioti.

The Theatre is reached from a footpath leading north from the hamlet on the 'dromo'. It is semicircular in plan, larger than the normal Roman model, and must be regarded as Hellenistic in date, much re-handled in Roman times. Close by 37 bronze tablets with Greek inscriptions of the III century B.C. were found in a stone receptacle; they refer to the finances allocated for building the town wall and other public buildings.

The Centocamere. This is an urban area only partially excavated. Some of the house foundations and parts of a water system can be seen, as well as the beaten-earth streets dividing the *insulae*. A stretch of the earlier town wall can also be seen. Some of the houses are thought to have been lived in by craftsmen, as remains of a pottery kiln have been found.

Of the two remaining buildings, the Sanctuary of Persephone and the temple of Casa Marafioti, little or nothing remains to be seen. The **Sanctuary of Persephone** stood outside the city wall in the valley near the Mannella. It has yielded a huge deposit of ex-voto *pinakes* (now in Reggio Calabria and Taranto) (see p. 181) and a dedicatory inscription to Persephone, as well probably as the magnificent sculptures known as the Ludovisi and Boston thrones. The **Temple of Casa Marafioti** stood near the theatre. It was unusual in style: Doric, with upper courses made of limestone to which was nailed a terracotta revetment. The V century *acroteria* depicted youths on horseback, their horses supported on crouching sphinxes, rather like the marble ones from Marasà, now in Reggio (see Plate 23). The plan of this temple is uncertain but it probably had a single row of columns down the main axis.

Plate 24 Birth of Venus from the Ludovisi throne (probably originally from Locri).

Papasidero (Grotta del Romito)

This is reached by taking the road from Scalea Marina, a short distance to the south of Praia a Mare, to San Domenico Talao and beyond to the village of Montagna. Alternatively the village can be reached by turning off the Autostrada del Sole near Mormanno. The distance from either is about 23 km. The cave is not very accessible as it takes about 40 minutes to reach it on foot from the village. Its importance lies in the fact that it has produced an engraved figure of a bull (*Bos primigenius*) strongly incised, with a smaller and more lightly incised animal below it. Of Upper Palaeolithic date, and comparable to the figure from the Grotta Romanelli in Apulia (see p. 149), it is thought to belong to about 10,000 years B.C. and is later than the rather stylistically comparable drawings of the so-called Franco-Cantabrian group in France and Spain. A bone point was also found in this cave, finely incised with geometric designs.

Praia a Mare (Grotta della Madonna). This cave is still a sanctuary much visited by pilgrims. It is at the south end of the town, on the east side of Monte Vingiolo. It was occupied at various times from the Upper Palaeolithic to the Roman period. The Neolithic and Bronze Age levels are important for having substantiated the sequence of cultures already known from the Aeolian Islands, and both Serra d'Alto and Thapsos style wares were found. There is an interesting diagram of its stratigraphical levels in the Pigorini Museum in Rome.

Punta Alice, near Cirò Marina

A few hundred yards from the point (the ancient *Crimisa promontorium*) near the tourist village, there lie the scant remains of the foundations of the Temple of Apollo Alaeus, which probably stood outside the walls of the small Greek town of *Crimisa*, about which very little is known. The temple was excavated by Orsi who found some small Doric capitals of the V century B.C. and an important marble statue of Apollo (now in the *Museo Nazionale* at Reggio, see p. 182). It originally wore a bronze wig, and its feet were shod with bronze sandals. Near the statue the quiver and arrows of Heracles are said to have been placed as a consecration offering by the legendary founder of Crimisa, Philoctetes.

12

Reggio di Calabria (Greek *Rhegion*)

Although Reggio was a Greek site of great importance there is so little of its past to see today that only a short outline of its history will be given here. Part of what may be the city walls can be seen near the Post Office in Corso Vittorio Emanuele, and in Via Torrione there are foundations of a small Greek temple. The *Museo Nazionale* is extremely rich (see below).

Rhegion was founded in the second half of the VIII century B.C. (716 according to Eusebius), by Chalcidians from Euboea. Its terrain and harbour facilities were so poor that it must have been chosen for its position dominating the Messina straits, and for the commercial and political advantage to which this would lead, for the Chalcidians were active traders with the eastern Mediterranean; as a port of call for ships bound for another Chalcidian colony, Cumae, and for the Etruscan towns further north, it would also be valuable. But in fact Rhegion was nearly always in danger from either Locri or Syracuse, both of which looked upon it with covetous eyes.

Fig. 26 Coin of Rhegion with lion's head.

After the famous battle of Cumae in 474 B.C. when Hieron I of Syracuse defeated the Etruscans, the worsening relations with Cumae itself and with Locri, and the growing power of Syracuse and Croton, led Rhegion into an alliance with Taras (Taranto). By the time of Dionysius's intervention in Magna Graecia Rhegion found itself uncomfortably wedged between Syracuse and its ally Locri, and when the native Lucanians pressed southwards and began to menace the Greek cities, some of these, including Rhegion, refounded the so-called

Achaean League. But Dionysius urgently needed the town both as a bridgehead and as a forward post for the defence of Sicily, and during a long siege in 387–386 B.C. he first starved out the inhabitants, and then dismantled the walls and built a palace there. He is also said to have built a wall across the isthmus between the gulfs of Squillace and Hipponium (Vibo Valentia).

After Dionysius, Rhegion fell into a period of political disorder. The native Lucanians and Bruttians were becoming ever more threatening, and eventually in 282 B.C. Rhegion asked for and received a Roman garrison. This prevented the town from sending help to Pyrrhus when he arrived in Southern Italy to defend the Greek towns. Ships and crews were provided by the town for the Romans in the First Punic War, and in the war against Hannibal it remained faithful to Rome and was rewarded with certain privileges. New colonists were sent by Augustus, and thanks to its key position in the straits Rhegion flourished throughout the imperial Roman period.

Museo Nazionale. Piazza De Nava at the east end of Corso Garibaldi. *Opening hours: Summer* (June 1st–August 31st), weekdays except Mondays, 9–1 and 3.30–6; holidays, 9–1. *Winter* (September 1st–May 31st), weekdays except Mondays, 9.30–4; holidays, 9.30–1.30.

Note that the Museum is always closed on Mondays.

This is one of the richest collections in Southern Italy, and contains finds dating from the Palaeolithic to the post-Roman periods. (There is also a collection, on the second floor, of medieval and later art and sculpture, with two exceptionally fine paintings by Antonella da Messina.)

The Ground Floor. The prehistoric finds are here arranged chronologically in five rooms. In the first room the earliest finds represented include the stratified series of *Palaeolithic* and later date from the caves of Grotta del Romito (Papasidero) and the Grotta della Madonna (Praia a Mare). Then follow the various phases of the *Neolithic* period, from the V and IV millennia of the early Neolithic to the early III millennium of the later Neolithic. Impressed wares from the village site of Favella della Corte and painted wares from Grotta St. Angelo III, Cassano Ionio etc. Then follow finds of the *Copper Age* (Eneolithic) of the III millennium, the *Early Bronze Age* (? 2000–1450), the *Middle Bronze Age* (characterized by the so-called Apennine Culture), 1450–1250. Lastly the Late Bronze Age (sub-Apennine) phase of about

Plate 25
Votive plaque
(*pinax*) from
Locri in
Reggio di
Calabria
Museum.

1250–950 B.C. and the *Iron Age* of about 950–650 B.C., the latter phase
coinciding with the Greek colonization.

Note the particularly important discoveries from Tropea (proto-
Villanovan urnfield), from Torre Galli, Francavilla Marittima etc. and
an interesting reconstruction of one of the Siculan-type rock-cut tombs
at Ianchina (Locri). This one contained 18 adult burials, some children,
and the remains of a new-born child in an amphora, as well as about
100 pots and many vases. During this period in Calabria both trench or
'fossa' graves and rock-cut tombs of that type were in use. The rest of
the rooms on this floor are dedicated to the more important discoveries
from Locri on the Ionian coast (see pp. 170–76).

From the cemeteries at Locri there is a rich collection of bronzes and
pottery, some of the latter imported from Greece and some of local
manufacture at Locri itself or from workshops in Apulia and Campania.

Plate 26 Sybaris—Remains of (?) theatre at Parco del Cavallo overlying ancient Sybaris.

The Sanctuary to Persephone at Mannella, Locri (see p. 176) has yielded some rare discoveries including an early V century bronze helmet with a dedicatory inscription to Persephone, votive terracottas showing the seated goddess, and above all the famous votive plaques or *pinakes* (see Plate 25) with fascinating scenes concerning the cult of Persephone. These were intended for hanging on the walls of buildings or even trees in the sacred enclosure, and were originally covered with a white slip painted in blue, red and yellow. The clay was unsuitable for very sharp modelling. Perhaps the earliest of these were made by Ionian Greek settlers, but most of them are strongly local in style and represent at least two generations of craftsmen. The scenes depicted are as follows:

Animals sacred to the goddesses, and cult objects (Cases 21 A.B.E. and 26B). The rape of Persephone by Pluto or one of his delegates (Cases 21 C.D.; 26B and C). The sacrifice and the ritual preparation (Case 23 A.B.). Fruit gathering and other country scenes (Case 23 A.B.C.). Preparations for the presentation of the nuptial *peplos*, the crown, and fruits to the goddess, and other processional scenes (Cases 23 C.D.; 24 A.B.; 27 B). The goddess's robing and hairdressing (Case 24 B.C.D.). Preparation of the marriage bed. The bridal procession (Case 24 C.D.). Persephone alone or with Pluto receiving presents from other deities, some of whom are shown separately (Cases 25; 26A; 27 A.B.C.). Persephone opening the hamper containing a male or female baby (Case 26a). (Students should note that there is a reserve collection of fragments which can be seen by arrangement.)

It can be seen at once that these plaques are executed with very considerable grace and artistry. While a few may go back to the VI century, the majority belong to the first half of the V century.

There are important terracottas from the revetment of the *Temple of Casa Marafioti* (Locri) as well as a terracotta *acroterion* of a horseman and sphinx of the late V century from the same temple. (Plate 24). In this room, too, are some of the bronze tablets from the Greek city archives.

Another room is dedicated to the *Sanctuary of Marasà* (Locri). There are some of the revetment terracottas (late VII–early VI century), a column and Ionic capital from the V century temple, the famous group of the Dioscuri (late V–early IV century) and some votive terracottas of Zeus etc.

Other rooms contain votive terracottas from the *Centocamere* area (Locri), and interesting models of sacred grottoes etc. from the Sanctuary of Grotta Caruso (IV century) thought to have been dedicated to the Nymph.

FIRST FLOOR. Finds from various cities of Magna Graecia, from Reggio, Medma, Hipponium, Metauro, Caulonia, Crimisa, Croton and Sybaris.

This very rich collection is soon to be rearranged in a more spacious layout on the same floor. Note specially the fine glass and gold-foil dish from Tresilico (4th century A.D.). The marble feet and head of a great statue of Apollo from the temple dedicated to that god at Cirò (Crimisa) are of the V century B.C., and the holes bored in the head and feet indicate where the bronze wig (see the next case) and possibly sandals were originally fixed.

There are VI–V century terracotta revetment fragments from the Temple of Hera Lacinia at Capo Colonna, Crotone (see p. 168). Part of a metope from an archaic building from Sybaris.

A very rich numismatic collection will be displayed on this floor, as well as Lucanian pottery, and an epigraphic section will be in the corridor.

Sybaris (near Sibari)
(for the Museum at the modern Sibari, see below)

Although nothing remains to be seen today of the great town of Sybaris which lies buried beneath the alluvial deposits in the valley near the mouth of the river Crati, this book would not be complete without some account of its extraordinary history and of the frantic search which archaeologists are making to locate the town before the industrial development, for which the site is earmarked, may obliterate it for ever.

The whole area offers enormous technical difficulties, for no sooner is a trench dug than it fills with water, so that recourse is necessarily had to the most up-to-date pumping methods, and a huge survey is being made with proton magnometers and other modern equipment. The result has been satisfactory, for recently archaic walls and fragments of archaic sculpture, almost certainly belonging to Sybaris, have been discovered at a site called Parco del Cavallo, on the left bank of the Crati, unfortunately at a great depth. Even so, the gradual uncovering of the immense riches of the town (thought to have been about 5 by 7 km. in extent, and to have had about 26 suburban settlements), even if only part of these can be uncovered, will be watched with the keenest interest by students all over the world. (See Plate 26).

Sybaris was an Achaean colony, founded in the later VIII century, perhaps around 720 B.C. It grew rich rapidly owing to its very fertile hinterland which produced corn, oil, wine, timber, and even had silver mines. To these natural advantages were added locally produced woven goods, silver-work and pottery. The colony's wealth was also derived partly from its position on the trade route between the commercial city of Miletus in Greece and the cities of the Tyrrhenian coast, particularly *Poseidonia* (Paestum), with which its relations were always particularly close, and it has been claimed that even Cornish tin may have reached Sybaris by this route. So, by the VI century, its territory enlarged after the destruction of Siris, Sybaris was the largest and richest of the Greek colonies in Italy, and there are many legendary stories illustrating its wealth.

There was, however, deep animosity between the Crotonians and the Sybarites—the former so austere and serious, and the latter so luxurious and frivolous (so frivolous that it is even said that they taught their horses to dance to the flute). Timaeus also claims that they invented vapour baths and that they took their chamber-pots to parties with them.

By the end of the VI century war had broken out between Sybaris with its huge army, estimated by classical writers, no doubt exaggeratedly, at 300,000 men, and the Crotonians with a far smaller army led by the great athlete Milo, and the result was an overwhelming victory in 510 B.C. for the latter whose loathing for their rivals was so deep that, according to Herodotus, they diverted the course of the river Crati to obliterate the city; whether such a feat could really have been achieved is doubtful, but the whole area is liable to torrential flooding, earthquakes and landslides, and these may have brought about the burial of the town.

After the final catastrophe several other cities grew up in the same area, first *Thurii* (where Herodotus died) and then the Roman *Copia Thurii*, and some smaller towns which may have been sacked by the Bruttians.

The Museum is in construction near the station at Sibari. It will house finds from the various Greek and Roman towns on the site, as well as important native finds from the tombs (large cairns of IX–VII century date) at Monte Pollino near the notable ancient centre at Francavilla Marittima. The earliest of these tombs contained cremation burials which were then succeeded by inhumations. They were accompanied by amber and bronze objects, bead necklaces, etc.

Vibo Valentia (Greek *Hipponium*)

Now, as in Roman times, called Vibo Valentia, Hipponium was a Greek city on the Tyrrhenian coast. There is an impressive stretch of bastioned walls to see, as well as the foundations of a magnificently sited Doric temple, overlooking miles of coast and sea. A State museum has recently been opened in Palazzo Gagliardi in Corso Umberto.

Not far away from Vibo, towards the delightful little town of Tropea, a flourishing indigenous (Siculan) centre has been discovered at Torre Galli. Its cemetery was found to consist partly of Iron Age 'fossa' or trench graves, and partly of a proto-Villanovan urnfield, reflecting settlers from further north. The finds from here can be seen in the museum at Reggio Calabria. Amongst them are imported Corinthian wares of the VII century which show that trade relations with the area may have already been established before Hipponium was founded.

Of the early days of the colony we know very little, but it was probably founded in the VII–VI century by Chalcidians from Rhegion (Reggio Calabria) and from Zancle (Messina). It appears to have been re-colonized towards the end of the VI century by people from Locri who valued it not only as a strategic port of call for ships trading up the coast to Cumae, but also as a useful outpost on the Tyrrhenian coast which could be reached overland rather than through the danger-infested straits. At about this time the first of the known temples was put up on the site of the present Parco della Rimembranza. Not long after, in about 480 B.C., we know from written sources, the Syracusan tyrant Gelon built a temple or shrine here in Hipponium, and this is not surprising, for he was a close ally of its parent city, Locri, and it may have been through Syracusan influence that Hipponium shared the cult of Persephone with Sicily. Many centuries later Strabo mentions this cult in these words: 'And because the country around Hipponium has luxuriant meadows abounding in flowers, people have believed that Kore (Persephone) used to come hither from Sicily to gather flowers, and consequently it has become the custom amongst the women of Hipponium to gather flowers to weave into garlands, so that on holidays it is a disgrace to wear bought garlands.' Persephone must have been identified with the pre-existing local chthonic deity to whom the earliest temples may have been built, and by the IV century yet another related goddess, Pandina, was worshipped at Hipponium, and her name inscribed on some of the coins.

As the colony grew in size and prosperity it tried to develop on its own and to liberate itself from the political ties with Locri, and about then the defences, which probably were originally constructed at about the time of Gelon, were first modified and strengthened. Further modifications may have been made in around 389 B.C. when Dionysius of Syracuse, fighting against Rhegion and its allies in an attempt to control the Messina straits, attacked and destroyed Hipponium and restored its territory to his allies the Locrians. But like all the Greek cities in Magna Graecia it was destined never to enjoy peaceful conditions for long. First the Carthaginians rebuilt it and brought back some of its displaced inhabitants, but afterwards left it to its fate. Then, in 356, it fell to the Bruttians who, together with the Lucanians, were putting strong pressure on the southern Greek towns. In 293 it was besieged and taken by Agathocles of Syracuse who built a harbour nearby at the present Bivona—a harbour which was to play an important rôle two centuries later in the war between Octavian and Sextus Pompey, both of whom used it as a naval base. But the Bruttians are known to have occupied Hipponium again after only a short interval, and in their hands it seems to have remained in a somewhat decadent state until, after 30 years in Locrian possession again from 260–230, the whole peninsula passed into Roman hands. Strangely enough, although during the Second Punic War Hannibal was operating intensively in that area, the historians make no mention of the town. A Roman colony was founded there in 192 B.C. and thenceforth its name was changed to Valentia, though after 89 B.C., when it was granted Roman citizenship, it was sometimes referred to as Vibo (a Bruttian version, maybe, of the Greek *Hippo*) and this is the form of the name used by Cicero who stayed here with a friend before going into exile.

In Roman hands it flourished as it had not had a chance to do for centuries. Dockyards and shipbuilding installations were constructed in the harbour which was busy with the export of timber from the Sila, and its communications were immensely improved after about 132 B.C., when the long coast road, the Via Popilia, passed through the town on its way to the south. Appian, writing in the 2nd century A.D., writes of Valentia as being one of the most prosperous towns in the south, and so it appears to have remained right through imperial Roman times.

The Temple in the Parco della Rimembranza. It is not necessary to enter the town to see either this or the walls. Coming from the more northerly of the two roads leading into Vibo Valentia from the Autostrada del Sole, just after passing a stone marked 1 km. to Vibo S. Onof. Filogaso, turn right immediately before some barracks, up a lane to the Parco della Rimembranza (sometimes called the Belvedere). From here, 500 metres above the sea, is a magnificent view right up the coast to the north, with Etna visible on clear days to the south and Stromboli and the other Lipari islands on the horizon. The great archaeologist Paolo Orsi was convinced that this site would certainly have been chosen by the Greeks for building a temple, and a small excavation soon revealed that his conviction was correct.

Only the foundations of the temple remain. It was a late VI or early V century building in the Doric style, with a pronaos, cella and rather long opisthodomus, and it evidently stood outside the walls of the city.

A few lion-head waterspouts and roof terracottas were found here and a number of votive statuettes of a seated goddess, possibly Persephone to whom the temple may have been dedicated. It must have been an impressive beacon for passing ships like the more widely venerated temple of Hera Lacinia at Crotone.

On the high land beyond the cemetery two other Doric temples have been identified, as well as one of the few Ionic temples so far known from Magna Graecia. In view of the colony's close ties with Locri, this is no surprise.

The Greek Walls (Plate 27). Return to the road again and take a small cypress-lined lane almost opposite, leading uphill towards the cemetery. When this lane bends right after a short distance, a gate on the left opens straight on to a fine stretch of the walls, impressive not only for their state of preservation, but also for their length of nearly 500 metres. These walls, which originally had a wide ditch in front of them, do not belong to only one phase; whereas in some places the masonry is carefully laid with rectangular blocks, elsewhere it appears to be much less competently built, perhaps in times of unexpected danger. Probably at least three different phases will one day be recognized here. The walls were interspersed with semicircular towers on square foundations, and the last of these marks a change of direction; as can be seen in the plan (Fig. 27), it replaced an earlier one. Some of the better-preserved towers had semicircular guard-houses with curved roofs. In front of one small gateway which is certainly a secondary modification, Orsi found a number of iron darts, some of which were still sticking into the walls, and were shot perhaps either by Agathocles's men, or by the Bruttians.

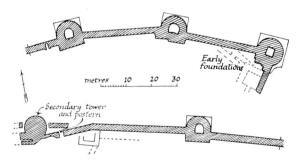

Fig. 27 Plan of the walls at Vibo Valentia (*Hipponium*).

Plate 27 Vibo Valentia (*Hipponium*). The Greek walls.

Whatever danger was expected, the builders of these defences were protecting themselves from the seaward, rather than the landward side, and their first enemies may have been the pirates in the early V century. Subsequently, under Locrian domination the walls may have been strengthened, and they were almost certainly re-modified in the IV century, possibly against or during the attack by Dionysius or the Bruttians.

6 · THE POTENZA AREA AND THE COAST TO THE WEST

Gravina di Puglia, Grumento Nova, Irsina, Oliveto Lucano,
Padula, Paestum, Potenza, Salerno, Teggiano, Vaglio Basilicata,
Velia.

This chapter covers the high country around Potenza, the very
heart of the area dominated, at the time of the Greek colonies, by the
native Lucanians. It also includes a stretch of coast separated from the
main uplands by a ridge of mountains and by the long valley known as
the Vallo di Diana, a dried-up lake bottom which is now under cultiva-
tion and which must have provided easy communications from prehistoric times onwards. It contains prehistoric remains and was evidently
used by the Villanovans of the IX–VIII century who settled at Sala Consilina a century or two before the Greeks founded their coastal settlements, and some thousand years or more later than the rock-cut tombs
in a field at Gaudo just outside Paestum—tombs whose contents reflect
contacts with Anatolia.

This whole area was exposed to many external influences from early
times. The Etruscans and their Villanovan predecessors penetrated it,
even if not very extensively, from the north: Greek influence radiated
first from Poseidonia (Paestum) and later from Velia, the home of the
great school of the Eleatic philosophers; and it is probable that tin,
some of it probably Cornish, indispensable for bronze working, was
imported to this coast. Both towns had been built to add stability to the
other Greek colonies such as Pithekoussai and Cumae which, as
described in Chapter I, had been established with a view to exploiting
the possibility of trade with the Etruscans whose metal ores were so
much sought after. These were the most conspicuous influences. There
was, however, also the contemporary but so far little understood culture
of the native Lucanians who, while borrowing much from the Greeks
with whom they came into contact along the coast, nevertheless retained
much individuality in their art and their way of life. The degree of their
Hellenization was, as elsewhere in Southern Italy and Sicily, in more or
less direct relation to their accessibility to the Greek colonies. The
Lucanians seem to have been a confederacy of clans speaking the Oscan
tongue, and ruled by chiefs or princelings living in defended upland

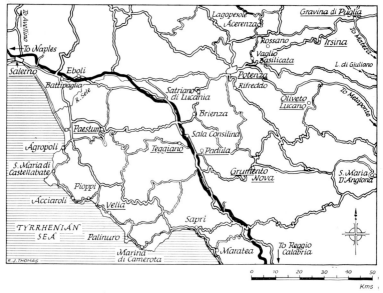

Fig. 28 Map of the Potenza area and the coast to the west.

communities. One such group has recently been identified to the north-east of Potenza, with its political headquarters at Vaglio Basilicata and its religious centre not far away at Rossano.

The Lucanians naturally aspired to conquer the rich and culturally more advanced Greek cities. They were sometimes successful, but they were repeatedly caught up in the various wars involving Romans, Carthaginians and Greeks, and often had to form alliances based on expediency.

The Museum at Paestum contains finds from the most important representative cultures in the area—the Copper Age grave-goods from the tombs at Gaudo, pre-Greek Villanovan finds from Ponte Cagnano, and the Greek discoveries not only from Poseidonia itself, but also the metopes from the famous Sanctuary of Hera at the mouth of the river Sele. Recently some highly interesting painted murals from V and IV century tombs have been added to the collections. These paintings are of particular—perhaps unique—importance in view of the light that they throw on Greek paintings and the influence they may have had on non-Greek art.

Gravina di Puglia

The name Gravina means ravine, and in fact the town overlooks deep clefts in the rock, caused by erosion by torrents. The nearby hill of Botromagno on the east side of the torrent was the site of an important Peucetian town, perhaps known as *Sidion*, which in Roman times became known as *Silvium*, a halting-place on the Via Appia.

The Museo Pomarici Santomasi in Via Lelio Orsini contains mostly finds from Botromagno. One room, the *Sala della Peucezia*, contains indigenous geometric pottery. The *Sala Apula* has early-Italiot wares and IV century Apulian red-figure pottery, some of which is decorated with sacrificial scenes, terracotta objects, toys, statuettes etc. There is also a coin collection.

Excavations have recently been taking place near Gravina, and inquiries about visiting them can be made at the Museum.

Grumento Nova (ancient *Grumentum*)

This site is of interest only to archaeologists. To find it take the main road northwards from Grumento Nova and turn right at the signpost to the rather unspectacular ruins, lying to the south of road No. 103.

At one time this was one of the main Lucanian centres. It was first mentioned in the Second Punic War when it was the site of two battles, the first in 215 when the Romans defeated Hanno, and the second in 207 when Hannibal himself suffered a defeat. During the wars between the Romans and the Lucanians it changed hands several times, and Seneca says that in 90 B.C. it withstood a long Roman siege. Eventually it became a Roman colony and had a spell of some prosperity during the imperial period.

The remains include parts of the enclosing walls, dated from inscriptions to 57 and 51 B.C., and an aqueduct, and further up the hill is an overgrown theatre, partly Augustan and partly Tiberian in date. There are also extensive bath buildings and an amphitheatre.

There are two important bronzes from here in the British Museum: one a relief of Hercules fighting an Amazon, and the other a warrior on horseback, archaic Greek work, probably from Taranto or some other South Italian Greek colony.

Irsina

There is said to be a small museum here, the *Museo Archeologico Ianora*, with prehistoric and protohistoric finds from the district, including Italiot pottery and bronzes.

Oliveto Lucano (perhaps the ancient *Callipolis*)
(of interest only to archaeologists)

To reach the ancient town site you must ask for the mule track from the village to Monte Croccia Cognato from which you can look out over the Ionian sea and for miles around. Here are the remains of the defensive walls belonging to three different periods, the latest of which is built in the Greek manner. Parts of the entrance and defences of the acropolis are also visible. To judge from pottery found in excavations, the main period of the town's occupation ran from the VI to the IV century, and it was certainly in touch with the Greek colonial cities on the coast.

Padula

The grandiose Charterhouse known as the Certosa di San Lorenzo, famed for its Baroque architecture and fine staircase by Vanvitelli, houses a small but important collection of local antiquities from the site of Pietra Chiatta at Sala Consilina where many cremation graves of Villanovan type (IX–VIII century) as well as a later, archaic necropolis of the VII–VI century were excavated. The earlier graves produced native pottery and bronzes, the later, some Greek imports and local imitations as well as many brooches and small bronzes. The series is continued by finds from Padula itself, starting with Greco-Italiot objects of the VI–V century and ending with those from a III–II century Lucanian cemetery. Note that only some of the finds are on show: the rest are in store and can be seen by appointment with the Director of the Museum at Salerno. (There are other interesting bronzes from tombs in this general area, from the Boezio property, in the Petit Palais in Paris.)

Not far away is a district called Fuonti where there are remains of a 4th–5th century baptistery mentioned in one of Cassiodorus's letters.

Paestum (Greek *Poseidonia*) (Fig. 29)

It is almost incredible that, apart from one possible mention in Renaissance times, the splendid Greek temples at Paestum were only rediscovered in the 18th century; for hundreds of years they had been hidden among trees and malarial swamps which, in the course of centuries, had developed around them. They may even have been partly standing in water. Now they are about half a mile from the sea, but were originally closer, for the coastline has gradually altered. The defensive walls of the town surrounded a rocky plateau in a fertile plain, well protected by the nearby mountains through which passable overland routes via Sala Consilinum led to the Greek cities of the Ionian coast. Today the special quality of Paestum lies not only in its splendid temples (never used as were so many others as stone quarries), but in the fact that it gives us an opportunity of visualizing a complete Greek town unencumbered by modern building, though modified and added to in Roman times.

Several millennia before the town was founded the area had already

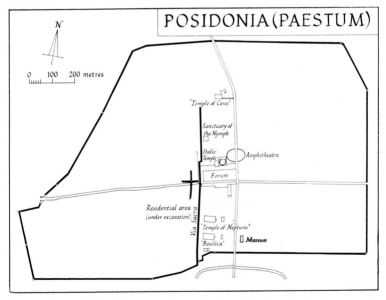

Fig. 29 General plan of Paestum from Geoffrey Woodhead: *The Greeks in the West*, in the Ancient Peoples and Places series, by permission of the publishers, Thames and Hudson.

been settled by prehistoric peoples. The important Gaudo tombs are in a field only a short distance away, and actually within the walls, between the so-called Temple of Ceres and the north gate (*Porta Aurea*), was another Neolithic and Copper Age settlement with painted wares resembling some from Lipari.

Strabo wrote that people from Sybaris (see p. 183) settled at Paestum at the end of the VII century or soon after. In fact a Protocorinthian vase from the site, and finds from the tombs, corroborate his claim. A date around 625 B.C. seems probable. He also wrote that walls were built round an area previously inhabited by native peoples, and given the name of Poseidonia. Even if, as some scholars think, Poseidonia was founded early in the VII century by sailors who also founded the Sanctuary at the mouth of the river Sele (see p. 202), it is clear that a Sybarite element must soon have joined them, and even after Sybaris itself had been destroyed in 510 B.C. the declining population of Poseidonia received a new infusion of vitality, perhaps the result of mass migration of homeless Sybarites.

From the beginning Poseidonia was destined to flourish, for it occupied a key position for trade with the Greeks and natives of the south of Italy, and even further afield with the eastern Mediterranean peoples, and the Etruscans who, by the VII–VI century, had pushed down as far as Sorrento. Even when the latter were defeated at the Battle of Cumae in 474 B.C., Poseidonia managed to hold its commercial position. It was growing ever richer, and, embellished with some of the loveliest of all temples and a notable treasure, the native Lucanians naturally aspired to possess it. Though well defended by its walls Poseidonia was not difficult to attack, and so eventually, shortly before 400 B.C., it fell, and its name was changed to *Paistom* or *Paistos*. Greek culture was almost stamped out, and even if there was a short respite in 332 B.C. when Alexander, King of Epirus, in answer to a request to help the Greek cities of Southern Italy, succeeded in defeating the Lucanians and Samnites at a great battle at Poseidonia itself, it was destined soon to fall again into Lucanian hands, and a further, and this time fatal, blow was dealt to Greek culture there, for even the language was suppressed.

With the rise of Roman power in the III century B.C. both Samnites and Greeks were dominated: a Latin colony was founded in 273 B.C. and given the name of Paestum, and it was obliged to provide Rome with ships and sailors when required. Throughout the ensuing campaign Paestum remained always faithful to Rome. The various Roman buildings in the town, the Forum, the Amphitheatre, bath buildings etc., testify to the prosperity at this time. But, as so often happened elsewhere, a fatal mistake had been made over the centuries in felling nearby forests: the river, as Strabo noted, became increasingly silted up with sediment of rocks and mud brought down from the hills, and gradually the site became more and more infested with malaria. In medieval times a few Christians were still worshipping in the Temple of Ceres (converted into a church dedicated now to the Virgin Mary instead of the Virgin Athena). But soon after that the forests and swamps encroached and finally hid it for centuries.

The town area, which is open from 9 a.m. till an hour before dusk, is now entered either through the south gate (from Sapri) or the north gate (from Battipaglia), the former bringing you directly to the two

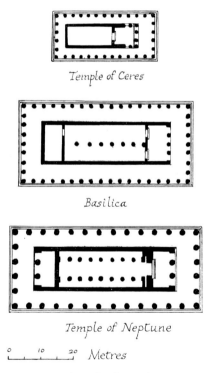

Temple of Ceres

Basilica

Temple of Neptune

Fig. 30 Paestum. Plans of the three Greek temples.

Plate 28 Paestum. The Temple of Neptune and the 'Basilica' temple.

big temples, the 'Basilica' and the Temple of Neptune, and the latter to the Temple of Ceres. The road from the station leads in from the east. For the three temples see Fig. 30 and also Fig. 33.

The 'Basilica', dedicated to Argive Hera, is the furthest south. It is the oldest temple here, going back to the mid VI century. Made, like the others, of local travertine, it has 9 by 18 columns showing marked entasis (curved tapering of the shaft), and flat echinuses. In many respects it is quite characteristic of archaic temples, but it has one unusual feature—a circlet of foliage or other design carved below the echinuses, particularly visible on the west front. It has a pronaos, leading by two doorways into the cella which was paved at a higher level than the portico. It was divided in two by a row of columns, three of which still stand, and which originally supported the timber roof-structure. This was the holy of holies where the statue of the deity stood. At the far end of the cella was the adyton, a small room used for housing the temple treasure. Outside the temple the great altar can be seen beside its *bothros* or pit for the remains of sacrifices. Many bases for statues stand

Plate 29 Paestum. Interior of the 'Temple of Neptune'.

here and there, and on the south side there are remains of small sacred buildings (some of the V century), where votive offerings were deposited.

The Temple of Neptune (Poseidon) stands beside the Basilica. Its name is imaginative rather than correct, for like the Basilica it, too, was dedicated to Hera: both stand, in fact, in a temenos in which have been found thousands of votive statuettes representing the goddess of motherhood and fertility to whom the Sanctuary at the mouth of the river Sele was also dedicated.

One of the most splendid of all Greek temples (see Plates 28 and 29), this is a Doric building with 6 by 14 columns, dating from about 450 B.C. Its design is very sophisticated. Its horizontal lines have a slight convexity to overcome the optical illusion that the columns lean outwards, and for the same reason the angle columns, or their fluting, are slightly inclined inwards. The columns have a notable entasis: in fact there are innumerable subtleties of measurement and emphasis. The raised cella, with its pronaos in front and an opisthodomus behind, is divided into three aisles by columns and pilasters supporting another order of smaller columns which once supported the architrave and roof. The metopes are plain, and small stone bosses below the triglyphs echo the nail heads of the original roof timbers.

There are remains of two sacrificial altars in front of this temple, the nearer of which was built by the Romans in the III century B.C. to replace an earlier one which ran the whole length of the façade. Here, too, grew the renowned twice-flowering roses of Paestum which delighted Virgil. To the left of the Temple stood various altars, shrines, inscribed stones and small temples, and the whole area between the Temple and the Roman Forum was once scattered with sacred buildings of the V–III centuries, all probably dedicated to Hera (equated with Juno by the Romans).

Continuing northwards past a Greek cistern you come to the grass-grown area of the **Roman Forum** (Fig. 31) which cuts right across the Greek sanctuary area. It was built in about 273 B.C. and only three of its porticos now remain. It was surrounded by shops and public and sacred buildings, and along the length of its south side passed the main east-west *decumanus* leading to the Porta Marina. At the junction of this road with the sacred way stood the curious bronze statue of Marsyas, now in the Museum.

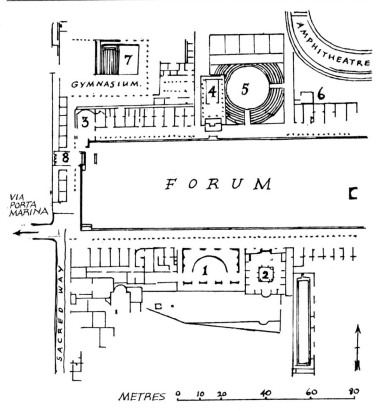

Fig. 31 Paestum. Plan of the area of the Roman forum.

On the south side of the Forum stood the *Curia* or *Comitium* and the *Macellum* or covered market.

The Comitium (1) is a complex building, as the semicircular part belongs to the republican period, but stands in a later, imperial, structure. Here it is thought were held the annual elections of the city magistrates.

The Macellum (2) is also of early imperial date, but it stands on the remains of a Greek temple.

On the west side of the Forum is a small building thought to have been a *Lararium* (8) (oratory to the Lares). Turning the corner you reach a *Sacellum* (3) or shrine, dedicated to one of the Emperors, then passing a row of shops you reach an impressive building on a high podium, the so-called *Temple of Peace* (4). This is one of the earliest buildings associated with the Forum, and its Italic form is clear from its orientation which, unlike that of Greek temples, has a north-south axis. As its cella was originally divided into three, the Temple may well have been dedicated to the Capitoline gods, Juno, Jupiter and Minerva. The present cella is part of a later rebuilding, carried out in around 80 B.C. The metopes which came from this temple show strong influence from Taranto.

Beside this temple, and in fact partly cut into it, is the *Bouleuterion* (5) or meeting-place. Originally, in about the IV century B.C. this was square externally with flights of steps leading up to the seating area. Near to this, and behind a row of shops, was a small building (6) intended, perhaps, to hold the city treasure.

The Amphitheatre has been only partially excavated as it is unfortunately bisected by the modern road. It belongs to the early 1st century A.D. It is unusual to find an amphitheatre in the centre and not on the periphery of a town, and the explanation may be that the eastern half of the Roman town, though inside the walls, had not yet been built up.

Behind the immediate area of the Forum and its surrounding buildings stood the great *Gymnasium* with its associated *Piscina* (7). The Gymnasium was originally a huge porticoed area with an entrance on the east where there are several small rooms. To the west it ended in a large apse, and in the centre stood the Piscina. The building does not all belong to one phase; perhaps it was first built in about the II century B.C., but its portico, at least, was altered in the imperial period, and there is evidence for its radical alteration after the eruption of Vesuvius in A.D. 79. At this time the Piscina was covered over. Of the *Piscina* you can see large stone slabs leading down to the bath with its central drain. Note the step on the east side where the umpire or starter of the swimming races stood. The big blocks of stone resting on pillars of the same rock may have supported a wooden plank stage for games and water sports, but its use is purely hypothetical.

To the west of the Forum the *Sacred or processional way* leads northwards to the Temple of Ceres: its paving, grooved by cartwheels, is Roman, but its line is that of the original Greek one. Continuing northwards you next reach a Roman residential area on the east and then a small temenos enclosing one of the most interesting structures in

Paestum, a late VI century **underground shrine** dedicated perhaps to Hera or Persephone. Some scholars regard it as a dedicatory sanctuary set up by Sybarites on their arrival in Poseidonia. The magnificent finds from this shrine, including some huge bronze vases containing honey, can be seen in the Museum. One of the vases bears the inscription 'I am sacred to the Nymph.' Only the pitched, red-tiled roof of the little building showed above ground. With one exception all the tiles are original.

The Temple of Ceres (more correctly Athena) is a Doric building set up towards the end of the VI century B.C. It has 6 by 13 columns and seems originally to have stood in a small temenos. Stylistically it falls into place between the very early Basilica and the Temple of Neptune, but it has one unique feature among the Paestan temples: its pronaos had 8 columns (of which only parts now remain in the museum) which were not Doric, but Ionic, suggesting that even at this early date in Paestum the Ionic style was regarded as most suitable for the internal parts of the temple. It had no opisthodomus. Parts of the trabeation and pediment still exist, and include fragments of the stone gutter with lion-head waterspouts. At one time this temple was used as a church and there are Christian tombs against the south wall of the cella. Outside you can see the remains of the temple altar and its sacrificial *bothros*, and an early VI century votive Doric column and various Greek fragments, some of which, like the column, are older than the temple.

The city walls, which follow the form of a low limestone plateau to enclose a pentagonal area, are particularly massive as the site had no natural defences. There were four gates at the cardinal points, in some places with corresponding bridges over an external ditch. Round or square towers protected the main gates and some of the posterns. All these defences have been rebuilt many times, and little or nothing of the VI century is now visible. The original walls were probably so badly damaged by the Italic peoples that they had to be rebuilt in about 330 B.C. and then strengthened against the Romans in 273 B.C.

The best stretch to visit is on the west, near the *Porta Marina* or sea gate. This part, which was rebuilt by the Romans in about 90 B.C., is especially well preserved, with guard-chambers and two square towers, both of which were built over earlier round towers of the V century. In front of the north wall a water-filled moat was dug in the IV century. The south gate was re-designed at the same time as the west gate.

The 'Museo di Paestum'. Visiting hours from 9 or 9.30 till an hour
before sunset. This very new and beautifully displayed collection still
in course of arrangement, contains finds from the town itself, from the
famous prehistoric tombs at Gaudo (2 km. away) and from Capo di
Fiume, and the Villanovan-type cremation tombs at Pontecagnano.
Of the greatest interest are the sculptured metopes and other architectural fragments from the famous Heraion or Sanctuary to Hera at
the mouth of the river Sele, a few miles to the north of Paestum.
Recently some magnificent painted tombs of the Greek and Lucanian
periods from Paestum have come to light, and are so fine and so
informative for the history of art, including Etruscan art, that special
rooms have now been built to accommodate them on the ground floor.

The Ground Floor is partly dedicated to the *Sanctuary to Hera* at the
mouth of the river Sele. Here stood a very small mid VI century temple
and a slightly later and larger one. Of these you can get a far clearer idea
from the reconstructions in the Museum than on the site itself. The
smaller temple had 36 metopes with reliefs which are sometimes only
roughed out and left uncompleted. They reflect a Peloponnesian style
with Ionian influences, and illustrate many of the best-known myths,
such as the struggle between Heracles and the Centaurs, and some of the
stories relating to the Trojan war. These metopes are less stylistically
evolved than those from the larger temple, which show even stronger
Ionian influence; unfortunately few of the latter remain.

The painted Murals. In very recent years excavations have brought
to light a number of extremely fascinating V and IV century painted
tombs which will always hold an important position in the history of
art. The best known of these shows a young man diving, an act which
perhaps symbolizes the departure from life to the underworld. It was
certainly, according to experts, painted by a Greek artist, and dates
from about 480 B.C. It formed one of the five panels of a tomb, and these
are the only classical Greek mural paintings from Italy so far known to
us today, though we know so much about the more durable architecture
and sculpture as well as vase paintings. These murals reveal the moment
of the rise of classicism.
  Equally interesting are some rather later Lucanian paintings
of the second half of the IV century B.C. painted when the town had
been for some fifty years in the hands of the Lucanians. The themes
depicted, as well as the armour and dress illustrated, are non-Greek.

Not so gay and lively as the tomb with the diver, these depict warriors, chariot races, funerals etc., and sometimes the deceased person is shown as a warrior on horseback journeying sadly towards the world of the dead. One of the warriors in these paintings is wearing an Italic helmet like one found in one of the tombs. In the scene of the four-horsed chariot race the painter was influenced by early Hellenistic art.

Not far from these tomb paintings are displayed the splendid bronze vases and other finds from the underground Shrine of Persephone described above.

The First Floor, dedicated to the prehistoric, Greek, Lucanian and Roman phases of Paestum, contains the unusually interesting and archaeologically important finds from the tombs at Gaudo; these are rock-cut tombs in the plain only 1 km. from Paestum on the Salerno road. (Turn left to the Masseria Gaudo and ask for the tombs, which are not easy to find without help.) So far 34 tombs have been excavated. They were communal tombs containing up to 25 persons, the old bodies being pushed back to make room for new. The culture they represent is so far known only in Campania and dates from about 2400 B.C. right through the Bronze Age. It is strongly influenced from Anatolia. Apart from quantities of pottery, there are ornaments, remains of necklaces, pendants, a silver ring etc.

There is also pottery associated with cremations of Villanovan type from Pontecagnano and Capo di Fiume.

Potenza

Thc seat of the *Soprintendenza alle Antichità* for Basilicata is in Via Vescovado, and the old *Museo Archeologico Provinciale*, just outside the town to the north, is now being replaced by a new one close to Viale Lazio in Via Piemonte. (Opening hours, 9–1; Sundays, 10–12). The finds displayed range from the Palaeolithic to the Iron Age and include much pottery and many Lucanian, Greek and Roman bronzes. Some of the finds from the Timmari urnfield are here, and there is a rich collection of Lucanian wares from the Cancellara necropolis and from the hill town of Vaglio Basilicata not far away (see p. 204). There are Italiot black- and red-figured wares from various sites, and important finds from the Garaguso necropolis including an interesting V century model of a marble temple with a seated goddess. Terracotta votive figurines etc. from Metaponto and other places. A small coin collection.

Both Vaglio Basilicata and Satriano di Lucania (the latter a few miles to the south-west of Potenza) have been the subject of recent excavations.

Salerno

The Soprintendenza alle Antichità for Campania has its offices here. There is also a museum, the *Museo Provinciale* which is now being reorganized in its new premises in Via San Benedetto. It contains material from Italic, Greek and Roman tombs etc.

Teggiano (ancient *Tegia* and Roman *Tegianum*)

This is a pleasant little hill town with many medieval buildings worth seeing and a small *Museo Civico* in the Church of San Pietro which was built on the remains of a Roman temple. It contains a number of Roman and medieval architectural fragments etc. The churches particularly likely to interest visitors are the Cathedral, Sant'Angelo (on the site of the ancient theatre), Sant' Agostino and the Gothic Chiesa della Pietà. There is a Roman mosaic in the Church of San Marco, and remains of a Roman bridge with reliefs and inscriptions are not far away. The life of the Roman town ended with its sack by Alaric in the 5th century.

Vaglio Basilicata

Remains of this early Lucanian town, whose origins may go back to about 1000 B.C., lie about 10 km. to the east of Potenza and you reach the site by turning steeply up to the village of Vaglio, from near which a lane leads up to the 'scavi' on Monte La Serra—a lane which is only passable with a car in good weather. The excavations, which are still taking place, have revealed about 7 km. of defensive walls made with well-squared ashlars, probably of the V century. The finds from Vaglio are in the Museum at Potenza and include some fine architectural terracottas of late VII century Greek derivation. Amongst these is an archaic frieze showing a battle between hoplites and cavalry, and also parts of an archaic Greek inscription. The indigenous geometric wares run from the VIII to the IV century at least. Remains of a Neolithic village have been discovered at the foot of the hill.

Not far from Vaglio, at Rossano, an important Lucanian sanctuary with about 30 stones inscribed in Greek characters but in the Oscan-Lucanian language has recently been discovered. It is thought that this area was the centre of a Lucanian federation with its political centre at Vaglio and its religious centre at Rossano, dedicated to Mephitis, a goddess who was trusted to avert pestilential exhalations.

Velia (ancient *Hyele* or *Elea*)

When in about 546–540 the Ionian Greek cities were attacked by the Persians, some of the Phocaeans escaped to Alalia in Corsica, but they were forced to abandon their new home, and they first took refuge at Rhegion (Reggio Calabria) and then founded their city of Hyele or Elea on the promontory at Velia. Founded on a site probably already occupied by people trading with the eastern Mediterranean, this was in fact the latest of the South Italian colonies, and it strengthened the line of Ionian cities on the west coast. The headland, surmounted by the acropolis, and now tunnelled through by a railway line, was once more sea-girt than it is today, for since Greek times—beginning indeed as early as Roman times—the sea has considerably receded in relation to the land, owing to the steady accumulation of alluvial deposits at the mouths of the two rivers which ran out, one to the north and one to the south of the headland.

In the VI and early V century the town became an important trading station between Massalia (Marseilles) and the Velian Phocaeans. Both were Ionian colonies, and Elea had much in common both in its planning and its defensive layout with towns in Asia Minor. Around the mid V century Elea, later described by Diogenes Laertius as 'an inconsiderable city, but one which was capable of producing great men', became famous for the distinguished school of medicine and philosophy (the Eleatic School) which grew up there at about the same time as the Pythagorean school was flourishing in Croton. This was during the so-called Athenian phase of the town's history when settlers from Thurii had made their home there.

The outstanding men at Elea were several. The main founder of the school was Parmenides, one of whose tenets was that he denied 'all change, motion, diversity and vacuum on the ground of inconceivability, and insisted on absolute unity, permanence and indestructibility of real being'. Deeply respected by Plato, he gave the town a code of laws. He was followed by his disciple Zeno whom Aristotle called the inventor of dialectic because he argued in support of hypotheses which he did

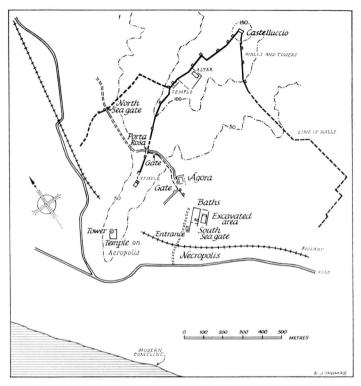

Fig. 32 Plan of the Greek remains at Velia (*Elea*).

not share. He postulated for instance that an arrow must remain stationary throughout its flight because at every moment it occupies only a space of its own size: it therefore does not move. It is not certain whether or no Xenophanes of Colophon, the poet and religious satirist, also lived at Elea for a time. He wrote a long poem about the town's foundation, and his religious doctrine was described by Aristotle as, 'Everything is one and that one is God.'

The history of the town can only be pieced together from the few references in the early histories: the rest will have to be filled in after more archaeological excavations have been carried out. During the IV century Elea was known to have been ardently Greek and it joined the Italiot league against the Lucanians who continually threatened it from the mountainous country inland. In spite of this constant menace, however, it survived sufficiently long to be one of the last strongholds of Greek culture in Italy.

In about 272 B.C. Elea allied itself to Rome and provided a quota of ships to the Roman fleet during the Second Punic War. After the Social Wars it was made a *municipium* and was apparently still flourishing in the I century B.C. when Cicero often stayed with friends in a villa here, and in fact it was in Elea that his dramatic talk with Brutus took place. The town was neither large nor rich for its hinterland was rocky and mountainous. Strabo wrote that the people were 'compelled on account of the poverty of their soil to busy themselves mostly with the sea and to establish factories for the salting of fish, and other such industries'. But gradually their livelihood became precarious for their harbours were becoming increasingly silted up, and although in Roman times a last phase of reconstruction was attempted, the life of the town was doomed. It was still trading in the Byzantine period, and later again a medieval watch-tower was built on the remains of a Greek temple on the acropolis. For centuries the site of Elea remained lost until it was rediscovered in 1883 by the French archaeologist Lenormant.

The long high promontory (Fig. 32) on which the town was built runs inland at right angles to the sea, and is divided into two nuclei, one to the north and one to the south of the long defensive wall which ran along the spine from the acropolis standing over the sea, to a small fort called the Castelluccio high up on the hill to the east. All along this spine the crest has been terraced for the foundations of various temples. Each nucleus had its own harbour (Virgil mentions several harbours in the *Aeneid*) and its own defensive walls joined to those on the ridge. The two quarters were linked by a remarkable road once running from the south sea-gate past the agora to the northern part of the town, passing under the famous Porta Rosa, the most remarkable gateway in Magna Graecia and beautifully preserved in spite of nearby landslides.

The visible remains

Entering from the south you pass first a part of the urban development on the right, with the south sea-gate once almost on the sea in one of the harbours. Near the gate have been found some inscriptions relating to a medical school at Elea and it is possible that there was an Asklepieion here. The sea-gate itself has an external square tower and it belongs to the first phase of the south-east stretches of the town walls, which, although not yet traced in full, have been found to date initially from the V century and to have been heightened and re-faced, perhaps because of encroaching sand-dunes, in about the III century B.C. Although the settlers from Thurii lived here in the mid V century, most of the buildings near the gateway are Hellenistic (see Plate 31A) and include a bath building. Shortly after passing this group of buildings a sharp re-entrant in the hillside on the left contains the agora once ornamented with fountains, and from here the road leads up to the Porta Rosa, a lofty rounded arch strengthened by a relieving arch

Plate 30 Velia. The viaduct archway.

Plates 31A, B Velia. (*above*) Hellenistic area.
(*below*) Remains of Greek temple below medieval
buildings on the acropolis.

evidently found necessary when it was heightened to act as a viaduct at right angles to the road below it, so carrying a track, bordered by defensive walls, running along the whole of the sacred area from the acropolis eastwards. The Porta Rosa (Plate 30) represents the key-point in the V century defences. Having passed beneath it you see before you an area whose character has been altered by landslides, and only archaeologists may want to continue further to find what remains of the north sea-gate. Rather than this it is better to follow a track up to the left to the acropolis where the remains of a medieval tower overlie the foundations of a very early Ionic temple perhaps of the VI century B.C., in the same area in which some late VI century Ionic antefixes were found. (Plate 31B).

Between the acropolis and the Porta Rosa excavations have revealed parts of the sacred area with small temples: to the east of the Porta Rosa is a small Hellenistic temple, re-handled in the I century B.C., near a once porticoed piazza with V century paving on which stood an altar to Poseidon Asphaleios. Still further east is a long artificially levelled platform reached by steps: here there is a big V century altar. Among the various deities whose cults are attested at Elea are Athena, Persephone and Apollo Óulios.

Excavations are continuing at Velia and among other work attempts will be made to locate and excavate the town's theatre and other public buildings.

GLOSSARY

ACROTERION	Ornamental sculpture at top or side angle of pediment.
ADYTON	Inner room behind the cella.
AGORA	Market place.
ANTEFIXES	Ornamental blocks on the edge of a roof to conceal the ends of the tiles.
ARULA	Small altar.
ASKOS	Greek pottery form.
ATRIUM	Colonnaded open court in a Roman house.
BASILICA (Roman)	Long apse-ended hall.
BOTHROS	Pit for votive offerings.
BUCCHERO	A reduced ware, black or grey throughout. It was made in the Aegean and in Etruria.
CALDARIUM	Hot room in Roman baths.
CARDO	Street at right angles to *decumanus*.
CAVEA	Auditorium of theatre.
CELLA	Room where the cult figure was kept in a temple.
COLONIA	Large town populated by Roman citizens— often retired legionaries.
COLUMBARIUM TOMB	Roman tomb with rows of small niches with the names inscribed over. Ancestral to catacombs.
DECUMANUS	A main axial street.
ECHINUS	Rounded moulding surmounting a capital.
ENTABLATURE	Architrave, frieze and cornice.
EPHEBE	Young man.
FRIGIDARIUM	Cool room in Roman baths.
'GRAVETTIAN'	An Upper Palaeolithic phase characterized by flint knives with blunted backs, and other flint tools.
HELLENISTIC PERIOD	Conventionally from Alexander the Great to Augustus. About 325–31 B.C.
HOPLITE	Heavily armed Greek foot-soldier.
HYPOGEUM	Underground vault.
INSULA	Block of houses between roads.
ITALIOT	From the Greek colonies in Southern Italy.

KRATER	Broad-necked Greek vase used for meals or for libations.
LEKYTHOS	Narrow-mouthed Greek vase for ointment or massaging oil.
MAGNA GRAECIA	Southern Italy colonized by the Greeks.
METOPE	Plain or decorated slabs alternating with triglyphs in a Doric frieze.
MITHRAEUM	Temple of the god Mithras.
MUNICIPIUM	Roman town possessing partial rights of Roman citizenship.
NYMPHAEUM	Fountain house or grotto dedicated to the Nymphs.
OPISTHODOMUS	Room behind the cellar in a Greek temple where the temple treasure was kept.
OPPIDUM	Fort, or tribal stronghold.
OPUS INCERTUM	Built with irregularly laid stones.
PALAESTRA	Gymnasium.
PEPLOS	A thick, sleeveless garment for women.
PERISTYLE GARDEN	Secluded courtyard.
PINAX (pinakes)	Plaque.
PISCINA	Bathing pool.
PISTRINUM	Bakehouse.
PODIUM	Squared platform on which Greek and Roman temples stood.
PRONAOS	Entrance hall to a temple.
SEPTAL STONES	Low stone sills dividing the passage of a tomb.
SICULAN	Of the people (*Siculi* or *Sikels*) who inhabited Sicily and parts of Southern Italy in the Bronze Age and later.
SIMA	A gutter to the roof.
SITULA	Large jar.
STAMNOS	Greek vase for storing wine, oil, salted meat etc.
STELE	Upright grave slab.
STEREOBATE	Stepped foundation platform of a temple.
STIPE	Votive deposit.
STYLOBATE	Upper surface of stereobate.
TABLINUM	Office in Roman house.
TAZZA	Greek cup.
TELAMON	Support in the form of a sculptured male figure.

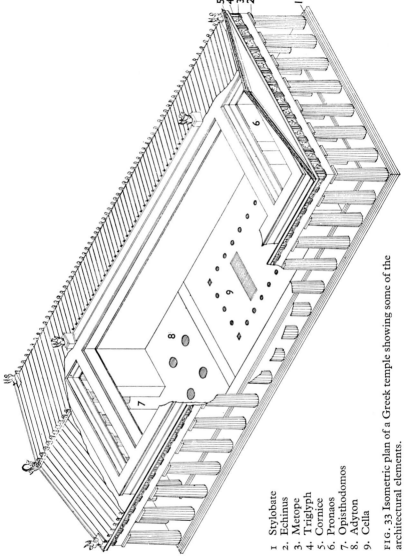

1. Stylobate
2. Echinus
3. Metope
4. Triglyph
5. Cornice
6. Pronaos
7. Opisthodomos
8. Adyton
9. Cella

FIG. 33 Isometric plan of a Greek temple showing some of the architectural elements.

TEMENOS	Sacred enclosure.
TEPIDARIUM	Warm room in Roman baths.
TERRA SIGILLATA	Roman glossy ware, red throughout and often decorated.
THOLOS	Dome, made with overlapping rings of stones.
TRABEATION	Beamed construction (as entablature)
TRICLINIUM	Dining room in Roman house.
TRIGLYPHS	Grooved stones alternating with metopes in a Doric frieze.
VILLANOVAN CULTURES	Pre-Etruscan North Italian Iron Age cultures, at least in part contemporary with the earliest Greek colonies. Characterized by cremations in covered biconical urns.

SHORT BIBLIOGRAPHY

General

DAVID TRUMP. *Central and Southern Italy before Rome* (Thames & Hudson 1966).

T. J. DUNBABIN. *The Western Greeks* (Oxford, 1948).

Italy's Life (ENIT), Vol. 26 (1961). *The Greeks in Italy.*

A. G. WOODHEAD. *The Greeks in the West* (Thames & Hudson, 1962).

G. M. A. RICHTER. *Ancient Italy* (1955).

D. RANDALL MacIVER. *Greek Cities in Italy and Sicily* (1931). (Out of date but pleasant reading.)

J. BOARDMAN. *The Greeks Overseas* (Penguin Books, 1964).

BÉRARD. *La Colonisation Grecque de l'Italie Méridionale et de la Sicile* (2nd ed. Paris, 1967).

A. FIORI. *Le Città della Magna Grecia* (ed. Privitera, 1965).

U. ZANOTTI-BIANCO. *La Magna Grecia* (Stringa, Genoa, 1962).

A. D. TRENDALL. *South Italian Vase Painting* (British Museum, 1966).

Among the classical writers note specially Livy, Strabo, Appian, Diodorus Siculus, Herodotus, Polybius, Virgil, Pliny, Timaeus.

Many important and up-to-date articles on various sites can be found in the *Enciclopedia dell' Arte Antica* (Rome, Istituto Poligrafico dello Stato) and the annual archaeological reports in *Journal of Hellenic Studies* and *American Journal of Archaeology*. The prehistory of Apulia is well discussed in Renato Peroni, *Archeologia della Puglia preistorica* (ed. De Luca 1967); and see also Bradford, J., 'Buried Landscapes in Southern Italy', in *Antiquity* XXIII (1949), 58-72.

Individual sites

Benevento. Sir Ian Richmond. *Roman Archaeology and Art* (Faber & Faber, 1969).

Caulonia. G. Schmiedt and R. Chevallier. *Caulonia e Metaponto* (1959).

Crimisa (Temple of Apollo). Orsi. *Templum Appollinis Alaei* (Società Magna Grecia, 1933).

Cumae. Monumenti Antichi. XXII (1913) and *Journal of Roman Studies.* LVIII (1968) 151.

Egnazia. L'Antica Egnazia (Soprintendenza alle Antichità della Puglia, Taranto, 1966).
Elea. See *Velia.*
Giovinazzo. Bullettino di paletnologia italiano (1967).
Heraclea. Forma Italiae (Siris—Heraclea) (Univ. di Roma, 1967).
Hipponio (Vibo Valentia). *Not. Scav.* (1921) and *Atti e Mem. Soc. Magna Grecia* (1928).
Ischia. Atti e Mem. Soc. Magna Grecia. I (1954), pp. 11–19.
Locri. Archaeology, XI (1958), 206–12.
Manduria. Atti VII. Congr. Int. Arch. Classica, II (1961).
Manfredonia (Daunian stelae). *Boll. d'Arte* (1965), *et seq.*
Metaponto. See *Caulonia* above.
Naples. Mario Napoli. *Napoli Greca-romana* (Naples, 1959).
Ordona (*Herdoniae*). *Archeologia* 49 and *Fasti Arch.* XX (1969).
Òtranto (dolmens). Peroni. *Archeologia della Puglia preistorica* (De Luca 1967), Nos. 2629 and 2630.
Papasidero (Grotta del Romito), *Klearchos* (1962), Nos. 13 and 14, and *Illustrated London News* (Dec. 1962).
Patù (Centopietre). *Antiquity* XL (1966), 253 ff. and refs.
Paestum (*Poseidonia*). Mario Napoli *Paestum* (1970).
Reggio Calabria. G. Vallet, *Rhégion et Zancle, Histoire, commerce et civilisation des cités Chalcidiennes du détroit de Messine* (1958).
Santa Sabina (Brindisi). *Boll. d'Arte,* XLVIII (1963), 123 ff.
Sybaris. Ezio Aletti, *Sibari, Turio, Copia* (Rome, 1960). See also Orville H. Bullitt, *Search for Sybaris* (Dent, 1971).
Taranto. Encic. dell' Arte Antica (1966) and bibliography.
Torre Castelluccia. Drago, *Autoctonia del Salento* (Locorotondo, 1950).
Velia. Mario Napoli, *Elea* or *Velia* (forthcoming, 1971).

An interesting short account of Parmenides, Pythagoras etc. is given in Bertrand Russell's *History of Western Philosophy* (Allen & Unwin, 1946).

INDEX